It's *My* Money!

A Guide to
Financial
Planning

for
Women

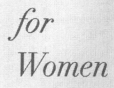

ELIZABETH SAGHI

It's My Money! A Guide to Financial Planning for Women
By Elizabeth Saghi

Copyright © 2016 by Elizabeth Saghi
Cover Design by Melody Hunter

ISBN: 978-1-944177-57-7 (p)
ISBN: 978-1-944177-58-4 (e)

Crescendo Publishing, LLC
300 Carlsbad Village Drive
Ste. 108A, #443
Carlsbad, California 92008-2999

www.CrescendoPublishing.com
GetPublished@CrescendoPublishing.com

A Message from the Author

To help you get the most out of my book, I have provided you with a complimentary "Personal Financial Organizer" booklet that will start you on your plan towards financial independence and security.

You can download this booklet at www.inalliancefinancial.com

Dedication

For Ricardo, Diana & Linda – thank you for believing in me.

Table of Contents

It's My Money!
A Guide to Financial Planning for Women

Introduction

After twenty-five years working for large brokerage firms, I decided to open my own practice because I wanted to help people discover the power of the financial planning process. Financial planning is a very broad subject and it means different things to people at different stages in their lives. And the emphasis is on stages, not ages. I wanted to write this book because I feel passionate about helping women become financially independent and secure. We all know that if you have control of your money, you will have control of your life. Being in control of our lives makes us happier in our relationships and more fulfilled in whatever we choose to do.

I used to think that most issues concerning financial planning and money management were not really gender specific. You earn money, contribute to your retirement plans, save at least ten percent of your income, invest well, don't spend more than you make and you should be fine. That's true for both men and women, right? Well, not always. Although women have certainly come a long way over the past few decades in terms of gaining financial independence, there are some concerning issues that still exist.

- Women still earn less than men for the same work... about twenty percent less.

- Women tend to work more in lower-wage, service, part-time, non-union and small firm jobs where they may not have adequate health care coverage or retirement savings benefits.

- Women are usually the caregivers for children and aging family members.

- Women are more likely than men to be single parents.

- Women take more time off from work and therefore contribute less to their savings and retirement plans.

- Women tend to live longer than men so their retirement needs have to be calculated for a longer period of time.

- Older, divorced women tend to have much lower incomes and higher poverty rates than widows.

- Women are more likely to be in jobs that are monotonous, with little control over how or when they work. This leads to increased stress which can lead to chronic illness. These jobs are also likely to be the ones that don't offer benefits like health care, retirement plans or paid leave.

- Women are more conservative in their investment styles than men which can translate to less growth in their retirement and investment portfolios.

I'll address these issues in the book and explain the ways we, as women, can protect ourselves. It's usually never too late to start planning but so much better if we start as early as possible.

During my career working at some of the largest investment firms in New York, London and San Francisco, I have lived through glass ceilings and pay inequality. For about three years during the 80's, I lived in Bahrain and worked as an institutional stockbroker for Merrill Lynch. Interestingly, I felt less gender discrimination there, as a professional, than while working in the U.S. In my personal life, I have suffered through a divorce by 'rushing to get it over with' and not thinking through the details, much to my regret. I learned so much over the years that I want to share so you won't repeat the mistakes I made.

This book is meant for women of all ages and the information is meaningful whether you choose to have a career, be a stay-at-home wife and/or mother, or both. I also hope it will prepare you financially so that when the unexpected happens, you feel in control and can weather the crisis. Financial Planning is not just about managing your investments. It's about knowing what you own, how you own it and why you own it – and then protecting those assets. It's about having enough money not just to pay the bills, but to live a comfortable life and not run out as you get older. It's about making sure you and your family get a good education and maintaining professional skills so that you're never at a disadvantage during your career. It's about financial freedom and security. I hope this book will serve as a guide when you start or revise your financial plan. I can't stress enough that it's essential to monitor your plan on a regular basis so that when life throws you those inevitable curveballs, or even when positive unexpected events come your way, you'll be able to get back on track quickly.

They say one becomes an expert after all the mistakes have been made. The word "all" is relative, but we do learn from our mistakes. My wish for you is to take something from this book that will enable you to make better choices and put you on the path toward financial independence. And remember, nobody cares more about your money than you do, so take control of your finances and live the best life you can.

Chapter 1
Financial Challenges Women Face

In a 1929 essay about 19th century women writers, Virginia Woolf wrote, "A woman might start out writing about one thing or another, but before she knows it, she'll find herself resenting the treatment of her sex and pleading for its rights." My intention with this book is not to step on a 'soapbox' demanding equal rights for women, but rather to point out that serious issues still exist today that can affect a woman's financial future and security. One might argue that financial requirements for women do not differ much from men's and that the general principals are universal, but women face unique challenges that require specific financial planning strategies.

Women live longer than men

Longevity is one of the biggest issues facing women today. The Census Bureau estimated that in 2015, the U.S. had four times as many female centenarians as male centenarians. About one out of every four sixty-five-year-old women today will live past age ninety, and one out of ten will live past age ninety-five. The fact is that nine out of ten women will be solely responsible for their finances at some point in their lives.

Since women typically outlive men, many may find themselves dealing with the death of a spouse. When a woman loses her husband or partner to death, words cannot express the emotional hardship she endures. She may not have been involved in making financial decisions with her spouse and therefore may be dangerously underprepared for taking control of the household finances. In most cases, when a spouse dies, one half of household income goes away, whether it is from wages or Social Security. That's a big drop in income and adjustments in lifestyle usually have to be made. A widow will then need to take sole responsibility for her finances at a time when she's emotionally overwhelmed. That is why the conventional advice given to widows is always, "Don't make any big decisions for the first year." My advice would be to have a plan beforehand and be prepared for the eventuality of being on your own. An essential component of the plan is to be involved in the household financial decisions as early in the marriage or relationship as possible, and stay involved throughout your marriage.

Women earn less than men

Another challenge that women face is earning less and thus, saving less than men. Census data shows that despite the important strides women have made in the workplace, their median weekly pay was still only about eighty percent that of men in 2015. For every dollar men earn, women earn eighty cents and this difference can add up to lifetime losses of hundreds of thousands of dollars. In 2016, April 12th was 'Equal Pay Day,' the day that symbolically marks when the average woman has worked long enough to catch up with what the average man made the year before. So think about it – we had to work three and a half months more than men in 2016 just to earn the same amount of money when doing the same type of work.

Yes, we've come a long way since 1979, when women earned just sixty-two percent as much as men, but we still earn less than men in many occupational categories, making it much more challenging for us to build wealth over the long-term. It's a mystery to me why this is still the case because women are now better educated than men, have nearly as much work experience and are equally likely to pursue many high-paying careers. Industries dominated by men pay more, but unfortunately women make up roughly two-thirds of all minimum wage workers. Maybe if there were more men in minimum wage jobs, the hourly rate would be much higher.

The Equal Rights Amendment (ERA), which makes discrimination against women unconstitutional, was first passed by Congress in 1972. By 1982, thirty-five states had ratified the amendment but it was three states short of the number needed to put the amendment into the Constitution. Since then, the ERA has been reintroduced in Congress every year. Even though women's issues now affect fifty-one percent of the U.S. population and ninety percent of Americans support the ERA, Congress has not once voted on it in the past thirty years.

Recently, an attorney friend of mine left her job at a prestigious law firm in Los Angeles to open a solo practice. She said that for the past ten years, she had worked ten hours a day, seven days a week until she discovered she was paid about twenty percent less than her male counterpart. She was extremely surprised and angry because she had always been told her work was better than her peers and she was on a partner track. In fact, her mentor was the Managing Partner of the firm. So she decided it was time to make a change. While it felt risky to move out on her own at first, her practice is now thriving, she's in control of her life and much happier as a result.

Women take time off to care for ailing relatives

Statistics show that women are more likely to be full-time caregivers than men, thus robbing them of time that would otherwise be spent earning money and saving for their retirement. Caregiving can also be costly and many women take on significant out-of-pocket costs for sick relatives. Professional caregivers get paid for their services and it would be great if health insurers found a way to compensate a relative who takes on the role of caregiver. Caregiving responsibilities make women more likely to leave jobs or work part-time which forces them to forfeit pension and retirement contribution benefits as a result. Many employers, particularly those that employ low-waged workers, don't guarantee that the position will be reinstated when the leave is over. As if dealing with an ill relative isn't emotionally hard in and of itself, the caregiver has the added stress of lost income.

Women are more conservative in their investment styles

Women have a tendency to save more, which is good, but they tend to keep their money in cash or low-growth savings accounts or bank CDs (Certificates of Deposit). They are less willing than men to take an added risk that will give them the opportunity of greater returns and growth in their investment portfolios. Being too conservative with our money and holding a lot of cash leaves us vulnerable to inflation risks. The cost of goods that we buy increases with inflation so we have to make sure that our money grows as well. Again, this is particularly important with women because we earn less, live longer and thus, have to make our money last longer. We'll discuss ways to invest and grow your wealth in more detail in Chapters 3 and 4.

Career vs. Family

Wouldn't it be great if we all had the good fortune to choose when to have children and when to stay home or give up a career to raise our children. For many women, it isn't a choice to remain childless – it just sneaks up on them while they are distracted by their careers. And for others, it's not a choice but a necessity to continue working after having a child. Whatever the reason, it's usually the woman who has to make that decision.

Although it's been almost two generations since women were told that "we can have it all," I think we're finding that it's pretty hard to 'have it all' successfully. Women still take up the lion's share of caring for a household and children's needs. Women in demanding careers find they need to put in more hours at work which means less time to spend with their families. And women who take extended leaves from their careers to care for their children, find that opportunities for promotion might be limited when they return to work.

Today, single motherhood is becoming much more common. According to the U.S. Census Bureau, in 2011 over forty percent of single mothers had never been married compared to only four percent in 1960. In addition, eighty-three percent of single parent families are single mother families while seventeen percent are single father families. I have the greatest admiration for women who have to balance their work life while raising children on their own, and plan their financial future. It's hard enough to do all three when you have a spouse or partner who shares the responsibilities.

The Impact of Divorce

Divorce can be a wrenching and emotional experience for all involved. However, women face an added challenge because statistics show that the average woman's income will decrease significantly after a divorce. Changing from a dual-income to a single-income household is hard and it also means having sole responsibility for your retirement income. After a divorce, on average, men experience an increase in income while women see their income decline. That goes back to the fact that women

11

still earn less than men so it's that much harder to make ends meet in a single income household. A divorce is an emotional life event, but the impact it can have on your savings and retirement should not be underestimated. In Chapter 9, we'll explore in more detail, the ways you can protect yourself in the event of divorce or separation.

Risk of Financial Dependence

When a woman quits the labor force to become a full-time mother or caregiver, it can have serious consequences on her long-term financial security. It's a big decision and not one that can be made lightly. The risk of financial dependency and the loss of all the benefits of working can affect a woman in so many ways. One spouse can become dismissive of the other when only one in the partnership or marriage is working and earning income. The non-working spouse can feel guilt or reluctance to spend money without asking for permission. This can bring up negative feelings of subservience or worthlessness. I know many non-working women that are married to successful men and still feel that it's "all his money." I ask them if they think their spouses would have been as successful if they didn't have someone taking care of every non-working aspect of their lives. What would it cost for their spouse to hire a housekeeper, nanny, personal assistant and cook? Whatever the cost, it certainly would have made a significant dent in the amount of money earned and saved.

The basic premise is that the more income a woman brings into her household, the more leverage she will have. Ok, you say – what if I've chosen not to work because I want to be a stay-at-home mom? I think it's terrific if you have the choice, but even if you're not working, take the initiative to get involved in the financial decisions of your house-hold as much as you can. Many spouses appreciate this effort as it takes away much of the burden of making financial decisions alone.

The good news is that women have made incredible progress, both professionally and personally, over the last fifty years. They are better educated, have careers with greater responsibility and increasingly, becoming leaders in their professions. More and more women are also starting their own business and as Forbes Magazine put it recently, entrepreneurship is "the new women's movement."

So to summarize, what can you do if you find yourself in one of the situations discussed in this chapter?

1. Know what you own and why you own it.
   Make a list of all your assets and know how they are titled. Keep up to date records of your banking and investment account transactions. Save at least five years of income tax returns and all the receipts for any household improvements.

2. Make sure that you and your children will be taken care of should anything happen to your spouse. Check to make sure that you are the beneficiary of your spouse's retirement accounts and life insurance policies.

3. List your monthly cash flow income and expenses and prepare a household budget with your spouse that can be shared with children when they're old enough to understand.
   Know what you're spending your money on so that changes can be made to your budget, if necessary.

4. Have all your essential documents in one folder, box or some sort of container that can be easily removed from your home in case of an emergency. These include wills, trusts, insurance documents, ownership records of assets, real-estate deeds, birth and marriage certificates, passwords for online accounts and a list of banks and brokerage firms where your money is held.

5. If there is someone other than your spouse that you have chosen to be a trustee, executor or guardian for your

children, make sure they know where all your important documents are located and who to contact at each institution.

6. The more financially literate you become, the more likely you are to plan for retirement, invest in the market, pay attention to fees and borrow at low costs. There are many articles and courses online that can help you navigate the financial industry waters. If you work with an advisor, ask questions so that you clearly understand the details of the financial transaction.

7. Look under the hood, kick the tires – know what your real costs and risks will be. Keep this mantra in your head – *'It's my money'* - whenever you feel hesitant to ask questions about a purchase or investment you don't understand.

Chapter 2
Organize Your Finances

There are basically three life phases where your money is concerned - accumulation, capital appreciation and capital distribution – and it's important to recognize which phase you're in before starting a financial plan.

The accumulation phase can be described as that time in your life when you're focused on accumulating all sorts of assets – a house or condo, a car, furniture, artwork, etc. Normally, this happens in our twenties and thirties where we invest in our education, start a career, have a family and buy a home. Of course, it doesn't have to be in that order and many women choose not to marry or have a family until later in life. During this accumulation phase we're spending rather than saving. Many of us take on debt to buy these assets and that might get us into trouble, especially if it's high interest credit card debt. Towards the end of this phase, paying off debt, saving and investing should start to become a priority.

As we move into the next phase, the pace of accumulating assets begins to slow. We move from spending to saving and hopefully, starting an investment portfolio with the goal of capital appreciation or growing your wealth. At this point, we are probably well into our careers and/or starting to think about funding our children's college expenses and our own retirement. This is the time to focus on paying off debt, especially high interest rate debt, with the possible exception of low-cost mortgages. Interest rates today are at historically low levels, so if you have a mortgage at a high interest, take the opportunity to refinance at a lower rate. High interest rate credit card debt can also be consolidated with reduced rates if you make the effort to talk directly to the credit card companies. Most of the time, they will work with you to lower the interest rate because they would rather have you pay something rather than default on the payment altogether.

By the time we are in our early to mid-sixties, we should be moving into the capital distribution phase of our lives. We are very close to or in retirement and planning to live off the assets we accumulated up to this point. As we build an investment portfolio during the accumulation phase, we'll need to allocate the assets to meet our individual goals and objectives. During the accumulation phase, we're looking for investments that offer growth so that we can stay ahead of inflation. As we start moving towards retirement, we'll want to reallocate those assets into ones that are less risky so that we can still get some sort of return even while taking money out as needed. We'll discuss this strategy in more detail further on in the book.

When I first meet with my clients, I ask them to describe what phase of life they're in, not necessarily what age they are, when we start to determine their financial goals and objectives. Opportunities and bad luck can happen to us at any time in our lives and thus, affect even the most well-laid out plans. So understanding the three life phases, asset accumulation, capital appreciation and capital distribution, will help you develop your financial plan.

Financial Fitness

There are 3 simple rules to becoming financially fit and independent:

- Spend less than you earn
- Avoid debt
- Invest your money

Let's deal with the first rule – Spend less than you earn. It sounds easy but it's hard for many of us because unexpected expenses can disrupt our plans. But it's a simple concept; spend less than what you earn in order to have money left over to invest. Ensure that your monthly fixed expenses are not so high that it undermines your ability to save a little from every paycheck. Think of increasing income as a good offensive strategy and decreasing expenditures as a good defensive strategy. Know your monthly cash flow needs by preparing a cash flow statement.

Cash Flow Statement

The basic purpose of a cash flow statement is to determine how your money is being spent on a monthly basis. Ideally, a year's worth of data should be gathered as some of your expenses might be seasonal, such as vacation expenses, property taxes etc. Paycheck stubs, check registers, bank statements, credit card statements, copies of paid bills and recent income tax returns are great sources to gather this information. At the end of this book in Appendix I, you will find a form that you can use as a guideline for preparing your personal cash flow statement.

1. Determine your monthly cash flow needs by making a list of all your income (from all sources including

salary, interest, dividends, rental income etc.) and your expenses. Subtract the total expenses from your total income and hopefully, this will be a positive number.

2. If it's not a positive number and you're spending more than you earn, go back over each expense and see where you can make some cuts. If you just can't make a cut anywhere, then perhaps you need to reevaluate the type of work you're doing. Can you get work that pays more? Can you take some courses that will get you work that pays more? Can you take on extra work?

3. Once you have some positive cash flow, the first thing to do with that extra money is pay off your high-interest credit card debt and begin to save a minimum of three to six months of monthly expenses as an emergency fund. Keep this money in a savings account where it can be easily accessed. In the event you lose your job or an emergency comes up, you'll have the funds available to pay your expenses until you get back on your feet again.

4. After putting together an emergency fund, start to contribute to some sort of retirement plan. If your employer offers a 401(k), 403(b) or some other qualified retirement plan, try to have as much as you can afford taken out of your salary. If there is a company match, have at least the maximum amount deferred to meet that match. If you're not sure about the appropriate amount you are able to defer, talk to someone in the Human Resources department. They know your salary history and you know your monthly cash flow needs, so together you can work out the right amount to contribute.

5. If your company doesn't offer a retirement plan, then look into opening an Individual Retirement Account or IRA. (We'll cover retirement planning in more detail further on in this book.)

6. After completing steps 1 through 5, you'll be ready to start an investment portfolio.

Debt

The next rule is to avoid debt. Yes, I know – there is good debt and there is bad debt. I'm talking about the bad debt, like credit cards, car loans, or any loans to buy a depreciating asset.

A depreciating asset is one that is not likely to appreciate in value, like your brand new car, which loses about 10% of it's value as soon as you drive it off the lot. Many credit cards charge high interest rates – sometimes as high as eighteen percent or more, especially if you don't pay off your balance in full each month. Credit cards are very useful but the best thing you can do is find one with a relatively low-interest rate, and try to pay off the balance in full each month, or as quickly as possible. Don't just pay interest toward a debt – it will take forever to pay it off and every month when you get your statement, you're reminded of that big lump sum you owe. Store cards or retail cards usually carry higher interest rates on balances carried over each month, so my suggestion is to avoid them. You should be eliminating all credit card debt before starting a savings or investment program.

Just to be clear, I don't mean giving up your credit cards because we all need one these days. I am talking about accumulating large amounts of credit card debt at high interest rates where you are paying off just the minimum amount each month. It will take you a long time to pay off that debt and virtually no investment these days will give you a return equal to high interest rate credit cards, unless you take a great amount of risk. Meaning, it doesn't make sense to pay ten or twelve percent interest on credit card debt and keep money in a savings account that won't even give you one percent these days. So pay off that debt first and then start your savings program.

Borrowing to buy a home is a good investment because, in most cases, real estate has provided long-term capital appreciation. Mortgage debt is good debt as long as you don't borrow more than eighty percent of the value of your home. We saw what happened in the pre-2008 period when mortgage loans were made with no down payment and/or adjustable rates that appreciated significantly three to five years later. Anyone could qualify with the "no-docs required" loans. It was pretty scary as I watched folks borrow all the equity in their homes to purchase another property with an interest only or adjustable rate mortgage. When the initial "teaser" rates were adjusted upwards, the payments grew unaffordable so that many were just walking away from their homes or the banks eventually foreclosed on the properties. Yes, the institutions can be blamed for allowing this to happen, but we have to take responsibility for our own actions as well. It's great to own a home, but buy one with mortgage payments that fit within your budget. Adjustable and interest only mortgages are appropriate if you don't plan to live in the house more than five or so years. But if this is your home and you're hoping to live in it as long as you can, a fifteen or thirty- year fixed-rate mortgage is the one for you. Fifteen-year mortgages will have higher monthly payments, but you'll be able to pay that mortgage off much faster and over the long run, will pay much less in interest. Try to get pre-qualified from a mortgage lender so that you'll know the amount they are willing to lend you and this will determine the price of the home you can afford. The interest on that mortgage debt is tax-deductible as is the property tax, and in most cases, your home will be an appreciating asset in the long-term.

Your Net Worth

Now it's time to determine your net worth which is a snapshot of everything you own and owe, at one particular point in time. A net worth statement is prepared by listing all the assets you own in one column and assigning a current dollar value to each item. This would include your home, other real estate, retirement accounts like 401(k)'s, 403(b)'s or IRAs, cash value in life insurance, cars, art, furniture etc. In the next column, list any loans, including mortgages, that you owe on any of those assets. Subtract what you owe from what you own and that is your net worth. Your assets are what you own and your liabilities are what you owe. Assets minus liabilities equals net worth.

If you own a business, you're familiar with cash flow and net worth statements. Be sure to include your business assets and cash flow when you prepare your personal financial statements. A consistent increase in your net worth, year over year, indicates you are in good financial health. At the end of this book in Appendix I, you'll find a form you can use as a guideline for creating a net worth statement.

Your Goals & Objectives

Finally, make a list of your financial goals and objectives, such as buying a new home, retiring in x number of years or funding an education plan for your child or grandchild. Whatever the goal, be specific about the amount of money you think you'll need and the time it will take to achieve that goal. The time horizon will become a crucial component of your investment strategy because it will help determine how much risk is right for you. The longer your time horizon, the more risk you can take. Review your cash flow statement, your net worth statement, and your goals and objectives at least once or twice a year. Make adjustments if there have been changes in your life such as a salary increase, a new family member, a new home or some other major event.

Preparing your financial statements may seem tedious at first, but it's such a good exercise and when you're done, you'll have a solid picture of the money you have available to invest and the amount of risk you can afford to take. All lenders will require this information and you'll also need it to prepare your tax returns each year. Excel spreadsheets are great for inputting and updating the data – especially if you keep a separate sheet for each year. Keeping your money in the bank seems, on the surface to be safe and risk-free, but you need growth to keep up with inflation. In order to have that, you'll need to save money to invest. If you invest wisely and not take unnecessary risk, you'll be able to meet your goals and become financially independent. Remember that not all decisions you make are financial, but they all have some financial consequence. There is nothing more rewarding in our lives than to be financially independent. Yes, money may not be everything but it sure gives us plenty of options and ultimately, peace of mind.

Chapter 3
The Basics of Investing

The odds are that at some point in your life, you will be solely responsible for your finances, whether you're single, married, divorced or widowed. We know that women tend to outlive their spouses, earn less than men and take longer breaks from work. According to the U.S. Census Bureau, the average age of widowhood is fifty-nine. Add to this the fact that a marriage has about a fifty-fifty chance of being successful. Because of these factors and many others, you owe it to yourself to learn as much as possible about taking care of your money.

I know many women who are quick to say, "I don't know anything about investing." I tell them not to be so quick to say that because they would be surprised at how much they do know. We run households where we have to budget our expenses. We make decisions about where to put the extra funds that we earn and we know how long and how much it takes to save for the things we want to buy. We have good instincts to know if we're paying too much or too little and we know the basic value of goods. These are the skills needed for investing.

Knowledge is key but sometimes too much information can confuse you. The financial services industry deliberately makes investment products sound too complicated for someone with little experience. Did you ever try to read the prospectus of one of the funds you're holding in your 401(k) account? If not, don't worry, you're not alone. For most of us, our eyes glaze over when we see all that "legalese," especially when it's in small print. In addition, no investment guru, hot shot stock picker or financial advisor can make recommendations that will consistently beat the market. So rather than buy the latest hot fund or that great new stock that your neighbor's son told you about, have a plan that suits your personal objectives.

As I tell my clients, you don't have to be a genius to invest well – you just need to know a few basics, form a plan and stick with it. Successful investing is not about achieving the highest returns – it's about meeting your own specific goals and having enough money to live the life you choose. You'll also discover that you don't need to invest in anything you don't understand or that sounds too complicated. My mantra when it comes to investing is "Simplify. Simplify. Simplify." Some people may be lucky to inherit their wealth but for most of us, the only way to achieve financial security is to save and invest for a long period of time.

Stocks, bonds & Cash

So let's start with the basics. Almost every financial investment product offered today can be broken down into one of the following asset classes: cash, stocks, bonds, real-estate, commodities, precious metals and collectibles like artwork or vintage cars. Cash, stocks and bonds are considered financial assets while the others would be considered hard or tangible assets. When you look at the details of any investment offered to you, it can be broken down to fit into one of the above-mentioned asset classes.

After you've paid your bills, there are three things you can do with any money left over; put it in the bank, buy something or loan it to someone. Buying an asset involves some degree of risk because you can never be sure it if will be worth in the future what you paid for it today. But the risk is worth it if the investment is later sold at a profit. If you don't want to take much risk but you'd like to earn something on your money, then make a loan to someone that you trust will give you back your money and pay you interest in the meantime.

Cash, Stocks and Bonds

Cash is cash! Cash equivalents include short-term securities that can be easily converted into cash, like Treasury Bills, Certificates of Deposit (CD's) and money-market funds. Commercial banks as well as brokerage firms will offer these short-term securities as an alternative to a simple checking or savings account. Other cash equivalent securities include instruments such as Commercial Paper and Bankers Acceptances, but these are used mostly by businesses and larger institutions. Basically, any instrument that has a maturity of less than a year can be easily converted to cash and fits into this category. These securities are usually considered very low-risk. The reward for taking on risk is the potential for a greater return, so if you have a financial goal with a long time horizon, you'll make more money by investing in stocks or longer-term bonds. If your time horizon is short, meaning less than three years, then limit yourself to safer assets like short-term bonds, CDs or money-market funds.

When you buy stocks, also called equities, you're buying a stake in a company. You like the business model, it's in a growing industry and you believe the stock price will increase as the earnings increase. It's like owning part of a business without having to operate it. However, the prices of most stocks fluctuate

25

so there is some risk investing in stocks. The overall market could drop because of economic or political forces, or the specific industry in which the company operates could be going through a bad spell. But the old adage, "No risk. No reward," holds very true in investing. Without taking some risk, you won't achieve the growth you need in your portfolio.

When you buy a bond, you're essentially loaning money to the government, a municipality or a corporation. That particular entity will pay you interest for the term of the bond and at the end of the term, you'll receive your initial investment back. Bonds, also called fixed income securities, involve interest rate risk which is the possibility that bond prices will decrease when interest rates increase. When interest rates fall, however, bond prices increase. So always remember that there is an inverse correlation between bonds and interest rates. At this time, we're in a very low interest rate environment and there is a strong likelihood that interest rates will rise in the near future. So the investment strategy at this time would be to stay in short-term bonds or cash and wait for interest rates to move up to a level that will offer very nice income on longer term bonds.

Precious Metals & Commodities

Investing in precious metals such as gold, silver, or platinum, and commodities are not for the faint of heart even though they have been around for thousands of years. I'm not talking about buying jewelry or buying coffee, bacon etc. at the market. I'm talking about buying these assets as investments. Normally, the person or institution engaging in these markets doesn't buy the actual commodity but rather enters into a "futures" contract to buy or sell at a specified price and a specified date in the future. Manufacturers, farmers and large corporations are involved in the commodities markets to hedge price changes in the materials they need to conduct their business. However, there are also "speculators" who will make a bet on a big movement, either up or down, in those markets. There are precious metal mutual funds and exchange traded funds (ETFs) which diversify the risk slightly, but generally these are considered very risky assets and more appropriate for institutional or very experienced investors.

Mutual Funds & ETFs

Most of us invest in stocks and bonds through mutual funds and ETFs. A mutual fund is an investment vehicle that is made up of a pool of funds for the purpose of investing in one of the asset classes. Each investor owns shares which represent a portion of the fund. A stock or equity mutual fund invests mostly in stocks; a bond or fixed income mutual fund invests mostly in bonds. A money market fund is actually a mutual fund that invests in short-term cash equivalent securities, as mentioned above. An ETF, or exchange-traded fund, is similar to a mutual fund in that it is a pool of money invested in one of the asset classes, but it trades on a major exchange, like the NY Stock Exchange, and has very low costs and more liquidity than a mutual fund. An ETF trades like a stock where you can buy or sell throughout the trading day, but a mutual fund price is listed once a day, at the close of the market.

A REIT, or Real-Estate Investment Trust, is a portfolio of income-producing real-estate holdings that distribute most of the income back to shareholders in the form of a quarterly dividend payment. Many investors like to own REITs because it offers them a way to invest in another asset class – real estate – without actually buying the property. Owning a property outright involves maintenance costs, property taxes, insurance and management responsibilities. If you believe that real-estate is a good long-term investment, then REITs will give you the advantages of growth, liquidity and income. A publicly traded REIT is like an ETF and trades on one of the major market exchanges. There are privately traded REITs that offer good income potential, but my advice to you is to look at them carefully because they are very illiquid and not suitable for all investors.

One of the main advantages of owning mutual funds is the professional management of your money. Most investors purchase funds rather than individual stocks or bonds because they don't have the time, inclination or expertise to do the research and due diligence needed in picking specific stocks or bonds. Another important advantage of mutual funds is diversification, because it reduces the risk of your investment by spreading it over a large number of securities. If a fund holds 100 different stocks and one of them goes down significantly in value, the overall loss in the fund will be minimal. If you owned that company outright and it represented a large chunk of your portfolio, you could suffer a big loss. It would be very difficult for the average investor to build and manage a diversified portfolio with a small amount of money. Mutual funds give you diversification even with smaller amounts of money, are liquid and can easily be converted into cash if you need the funds.

You can make money from mutual funds in several ways:

1. Income is earned from dividends in stock funds and from interest in bond funds. Once a year, the fund pays shareholders a distribution that consists of nearly all the income it's received.

2. When the fund sells stock that has appreciated in value, they pass on the capital gains to shareholders in the form of a distribution. However, be aware that capital gains distributions are taxable, so watch out for high trading volumes in funds if you are concerned about the tax impact.

3. When the holdings within a fund increase in value, the price of the mutual fund shares go up and you can sell them at a profit. Mutual fund prices are quoted after the

close of trading each day and the price you can sell or buy at is called the "Net Asset Value."

Fees and Expenses

Managing a mutual fund can be an expensive proposition. Fund managers are usually skilled and experienced investment professionals who command high salaries. Marketing the fund and administrative functions like producing investor statements are also costly. These expenses are passed on to the investor and can vary widely from one fund to another. When deciding on which fund to buy, always look at the "expense ratio," as high expenses can have negative long-term consequences in your portfolio. Every dollar you spend on these fees is money that has no opportunity to grow for you in the long-term. For example, if a mutual fund's expense ratio is one percent, then for every $10,000 of shares that you buy, only $9,900 is actually being invested. Expenses will affect the annual returns and performance of your investment portfolio.

Index Funds

An Index Fund is a type of mutual fund that matches the underlying components of a market index, such as the Standard & Poor's 500 Index. They are also referred to as "passive" funds because they consist of and track all the stocks within a specific index. They are not "actively" managed and therefore don't have the high expenses associated with professional managers.

They also don't incur trading fees because the only time a stock is bought or sold is when it's added or deleted from that index. The less trading that is done means it's more tax-efficient because you're not paying capital gains each time an appreciated stock is sold within the fund. Your capital gains tax is paid when you actually sell the fund and it has increased in value.

Warren Buffet, the founder of Berkshire Hathaway, and considered one of the most astute and successful investors of our time, set up a trust for his wife's estate and has directed that most of it be invested in a low-cost S&P 500 index fund. He was quoted as saying; *"My advice to the trustee could not be more simple. Put 10% of the cash in short-term government bonds and 90% in a very low-cost S&P 500 index fund, like Vanguard. I believe the trust's long-term results from this policy will be superior to those attained by most investors – whether pension funds, institutions, or individuals – who employ high-fee managers."*

Each mutual fund and ETF has a unique symbol. For example, the Vanguard S&P 500 Index Admiral Fund's symbol is VFIAX. Punching the symbols into your computer on a site like Google Finance or Yahoo Finance, will give you the latest prices and a description of that particular fund. Along with much information, you can determine if it's a stock or bond mutual fund, what the top security holdings are within the fund, a description of the portfolio managers and their investment style, and the expense ratios.

Some of the more common indexes include:

- Standard & Poor's 500) – includes the 500 largest companies in the U.S.

- Dow Jones Industrials – made up of 30 U.S. companies, each a leader in its' industry.

- Wilshire 5000 – this is probably the most comprehensive index as it tracks all the publicly traded companies in the U.S. (penny stocks and very small companies are excluded).

- NASDAQ 100 – includes the 100 largest technology companies in the U.S.

- MSCI EAFE – includes a selection of stocks from 21 developed countries, but excludes those from the U.S.

and Canada. The EAFE acronym stands for Europe, Australasia and Far East.

There are many other indices and you can find the names and more details on each at http://www.world-stock-exchanges.net/indices.html

Dividends

Many established companies pay dividends to their shareholders. Dividends are declared from net profits so a company that pays a dividend is usually doing well. There are exceptions, of course, but in general a dividend is an indication of a healthy company, particularly if that company has increased its' dividends consistently over the years.

If you buy a stock or a mutual fund that pays dividends and you reinvest those dividend payments back into shares of the stock or the fund, you'll earn additional dividends on the reinvested money. It's similar to compounding as described below. I usually recommend that my clients reinvest their dividends back into shares of the company or the fund. In the past 25 years, forty percent of stock market returns have come from dividends. For example, if the "total return" on your fund during that time was 6%, then 2.4% came from dividends and 3.6% came from the share price increase. I think that's a remarkable statistic and the best argument for concentrating your investment portfolio on investments that pay dividends.

The Power of Compounding

Compounding is the ability of an investment to generate earnings which are then reinvested in order to generate their own earnings. With compound interest, you earn interest on the money you save and on the interest that money earns. For example: You deposit $10,000 in a savings account that pays 5% per year. If you reinvest those interest payments each year, over 10 years your initial investment of $10,000 will grow to $16,289. If you don't reinvest the interest and use that money for other purposes, your investment in 10 years will still only be worth $10,000. That is the power of compounding.

Risk Tolerance

The purpose of a risk analysis to determine your specific risk profile or tolerance level, is to help you put together the investment strategy that makes the most sense for you. It also determines how much of your portfolio should be in stocks, as they are a higher risk asset class than bonds. If your time horizon is relatively short-term, you should be investing more conservatively. If you have a long-term time horizon, you can afford to take more risk. In addition to the time factor, your net worth and risk capital should also be taken into consideration. We've talked about net worth (assets minus liabilities). Risk capital is the money you can afford to lose – in other words, if you lost that money, how much of a difference would it make in your lifestyle. Think about what it would take to retrieve the amount lost. If your investment portfolio declined by fifty percent, it would take a return of one-hundred percent just to get back to even.

This is never an exact science but there are several questions you should ask yourself (and be as honest as possible with your answers) that will lead you to the portfolio that contains the right combination of investment classes best suited to your situation. For example:

1. How comfortable am I investing in stocks or stock mutual funds?
2. When will I need the money I'm investing?
3. How much am I prepared to lose?
4. What are my monthly income needs?

5. What is my family situation and what are my responsibilities to them?

6. What is my ultimate financial goal?

7. Can I do this myself or should I seek the help of a financial advisor?

There are a number of websites that have questionnaires to fill out which will help you determine your risk tolerance. One of the better ones is found on Vanguard's site at https://personal.vanguard.com/us/FundsInvQuestionnaire.

Purchasing Power

One of my mother's closest friends is now 96 years old. She was married to a successful businessman and enjoyed a wonderful life with him until he died when she was about 70. She thought she had enough money to last the rest of her life based on her monthly expenses and cash flow needs at that time. What she didn't plan for was rising costs and the increase in her living expenses due to inflation. She moved to San Francisco after her husband died and rented a condominium, rather than buying one. Even with rent control in that city, her rent alone had almost doubled in 20 years. All her other costs, particularly the out-of-pocket medical expenses had increased as well. The sad ending is that she ran out of money by the time she was 90 and had to move to a skilled nursing facility that was covered by Medicaid and her Social Security payments. Whenever I see her now, she tells me, "I thought I would be ok, but I simply ran out of money because I never planned to live this long."

Purchasing power is the value of the amount of goods and services one dollar will buy. Inflation decreases the value of what one dollar will buy. For example, the cost of a first-class postage stamp in 1980 was 15 cents – today that stamp costs 49 cents. When I went to college back in the seventies, one year of tuition cost $5,000 and that was a private university. Today, that same university charges over $45,000 per year. We all know how health care and housing costs have also risen substantially over the years. In order to keep up with inflationary costs, you have to have growth in your investment portfolios which means buying stocks or stock mutual funds, but that entails some risk. Women are generally good about saving money, but sometimes we tend to be too cautious about taking risks. Men generally tend to view investing as a game while women are much more goal-oriented, but in order to reach our goals and pay for them, we need to make our money grow. Today, we are in a low-interest rate environment, so while keeping your money in a savings account or a CD can seem risk-free, it also prevents you from growing your assets adequately to keep up with inflation. Purchasing power risk should always be taken into consideration when putting together a financial plan or investment portfolio.

As we said earlier, stocks produce growth in a portfolio, so they are a good inflation hedge and minimize the purchasing power risk. Bonds give you income but will generally decrease in value as interest rates increase. The balance of stocks and bonds in your portfolio will depend on your age, the phase of life you're in and the risk tolerance specific to your personal situation. The younger you are; the more stocks you should have in your portfolio because you want your money to grow. The closer you are to retirement, the more bonds you should be holding because they are less risky and will give you more income. However, even in retirement you should still have a certain percentage in growth stocks in order to stay ahead of inflation. Allocating your assets is an important investment strategy and we'll discuss that more in the next chapter.

If you don't have much experience in investing, this chapter might be confusing to you. It is difficult to condense the subject into just a few pages, but don't feel intimidated at all.

The best way to learn about investing is to actually invest. You'll learn as you go along and you'll find that it's not really that complicated, after all. And a little help along the way from a trusted advisor would be good too.

Chapter 4
Growing Your Wealth

What does wealth mean to you? When we talk about wealth, many of us think of large mansions, fancy cars, private jets or vacations in exotic locations. It always amazes me when I see the growing list of billionaires in Forbes magazines' annual survey because it makes a million dollars seem like small change these days. And of course, we hear more and more about the growing income discrepancy between the "one-per centers" and everyone else. But I think that for most of us, real wealth comes in the things that are most meaningful to us, like family, friends and good health. Money isn't everything in life, but it does give us options and the ability to spend time doing the things we enjoy with the people we care about most.

A good investment strategy may not make you a billionaire, but it will give you that peace of mind that comes with financial security. I believe we have wealth when we can maintain our lifestyle without ever running out of money. Clearly, everyone has different lifestyles and some need more than others. So determine where you'd like to be in your life and what it will cost you to get there. Be specific about your goals and have a timeline, if possible. For example, if one of your financial goals is to finance your child's college education, then depending on the age of your child, you can calculate how much you'll need, when you'll need it and what you'll need to invest to get there.

One of the most successful investors in the history of the U.S. was Benjamin Graham, a professor of finance at Columbia University and a mentor of Warren Buffet, another extremely successful investor in this country. Graham was known as the father of "value investing" and if you're so inclined, I would highly recommend reading his book, "The Intelligent Investor." It was written years ago but I still think it's one of the best investment strategy books out there. His basic premise was to buy low and sell high, but he was also adamant about understanding what you were buying. He liked to buy stocks that were undervalued, in that there was some temporary blip or anomaly that made the price fall, but the long-term prospects were good. If you're not sure what you're investing in, either ask more questions, learn more about it or just simply move on to something else that you do understand.

Benjamin Graham was also an advocate for long-term investing, rather than short-term trading. Patience is a virtue when it comes to investing, so keep that in mind as you put together your investment plan. One of my roles as a financial planner is to help my clients stay on track with their plans and not panic or get greedy with sudden, volatile swings in the market. Yes, sometimes we do make changes to a plan, but we discuss it calmly, try not to act irrationally and make sure the changes fit into the overall strategy to meet goals and objectives.

In the previous chapters, we discussed the ways to organize your finances so that you can have money to invest. An investment strategy is not just about getting the highest returns; it's about achieving your personal goals. We all have a different relationship with money that is ingrained in us from our childhood experiences. Some people believe that money will solve all their problems. Others believe that it's a status symbol and if you have lots of money, it must mean that you're smarter and more important. Still others are very secretive about their money or very frugal in their spending habits. Everyone has different reasons for investing but by understanding where you are now and where you need to go, you can manage your money in a systematic way. Before beginning to invest, have a plan that is based on the following principals:

1. *Suitable asset allocation* – What is the time horizon of the portfolio, i.e. how long before you will need the money? Determine how much risk you are willing to take with your investments. What is your risk tolerance, i.e. how much can you afford to lose? The longer the time horizon, the more risk you can take. Most of us aren't as much risk-averse as we are loss-averse, so determining how much we can realistically stand to lose is an important consideration. Stocks are riskier than bonds, but they offer more growth potential. The longer your time horizon, the greater percentage you should have in stocks. The closer you are to needing the money, the more you should have in short-term bonds or cash equivalents that offer little risk.

2. *Cost effective implementation* - Take a look at the fees that mutual funds charge...and they all do, even if hidden within the fund. Some charge upfront sales charges and some impose a back-end fee if you sell before a specific period of time. When you're looking at the details of a mutual fund, look closely at the "expense ratio" that will be included in the description of the fund. This is the percentage that is deducted from your account each year to pay for management fees and marketing costs, including commissions. The higher the expense ratio, the lower your return will be over time.

3. *Rebalancing* – Over time, one sector of the market or an asset class might outperform another and portfolios will drift away from your original asset allocation model. The original weighting of stocks, bonds and cash might now be skewed heavily in one area, depending on the performance of individual assets in your portfolio. You will need to adjust the balance by selling some of the investments that have outperformed and purchase more of those that have underperformed. It might sound counterintuitive to you, but it is really a very effective long-term investment strategy.

4. *Disciplined Approach* – Strategies like rebalancing and staying the course sound simple in theory, but sometimes human instinct pulls us to do the exact opposite of what we should be doing. For example, many people panic when the market drops significantly and the last thing they want to do is buy or invest more assets. But that is exactly what they should be doing. Conversely, when everyone is touting the 'latest and greatest' investment, it should be a red flag that signals a time to sell. Remember the often quoted saying, "Buy Low. Sell High." Keep that as a mantra in your head when you are investing your money.

5. *Tax Optimization* – When buying or selling an investment, you will want to take into consideration the tax consequences. Almost every financial transaction in our lives has some sort of taxable impact. Retirement accounts might be funded with pre-tax dollars and the money grows "tax-deferred," but you will have tax consequences when you begin to withdraw that money. It does, however, make sense to hold taxable bonds and dividend paying stocks in retirement accounts because interest and dividends grow tax-deferred. If you held them in a non-retirement account, you would have to pay tax each year on the interest and dividends earned.

Interest is taxed at ordinary income tax rates while qualified dividends are taxed at a fifteen percent rate.

We've heard of stock market traders that make a "killing" day-trading the markets. I'm sure some have made lots of money, but what you don't hear about is the taxes they have to pay on each profitable trade. In addition, high trading fees can eat up much of their investment gains. Short-term (less than one year) profits are taxed at ordinary income tax rates, which are the highest rates currently in place. A good investment strategy would be long-term, meaning greater than one year because long-term profits are taxed at capital gains rates, which are much lower. Tax rates do change but in 2015, the capital gains rates were as follows: If you're in the 10% to 15% tax bracket for ordinary income, then the rate is 0%. If you're in the 25% to 35% tax bracket, then your rate would be 15%. The maximum long-term capital gains rate at this time is 20%.

Diversification

Diversifying your assets doesn't mean buying a little bit of everything. Rather, it is an investment strategy that reduces risk by allocating your funds into different asset classes, different industries, different geographic locations and other categories. The basic premise is that you may be able to maximize returns by investing in different areas that might each react differently to the same event. While diversification does not guarantee against loss, it can minimize the risk of loss.

There are some risks that cannot be diversified, like inflation or interest rate risk, also called "systematic" or market risk. This is a risk that affects all industries so it can't be reduced or eliminated with diversification – it's just something we have to accept as investors. However, "unsystematic" risk such as business risk that affects a certain company or industry can be reduced through diversification. So the bottom line here is, "Don't put all your eggs in one basket" and have a good asset allocation strategy in place before you begin investing.

Target Date Funds

I'd like to write a few words about Target Date Funds because they are increasingly being offered to participants in company sponsored retirement plans.

Target date funds are mutual funds that are intended to be all-in-one investing solutions, capable of getting you all the way to retirement. They typically don't try to produce market-beating returns, but can provide an appropriate mix of stocks and bonds based on your age and your retirement date. Also called Lifecycle, Dynamic Risk or Age-Based funds, they provide automatic rebalancing by gradually increasing the proportion of bonds and cash as you get older.

The "target date" you choose is the one closest to the date of your planned retirement when you'll need those funds. For example, if you are thirty-five years old and plan to retire in thirty years, your target-date would be 2047. As you get closer to your retirement date, the assets in the fund will become less and less risky. Bond funds will replace stock funds. Target date funds simplify the process of investing the money in your retirement account if you aren't inclined to research the other choices of mutual funds available in your plan. Many times, they are the default option in a company-sponsored plan as well. This means that if you don't make an election as to where you'd like your salary deferrals, or your employer contributions to go, then they will automatically go into a target-date fund that is appropriate for your age group.

Professional Money Management

Money managers can be individuals or institutions like banks or businesses, that are responsible for managing the investment portfolios of individuals or institutional investors such as pension funds, endowment funds, etc. Money management firms have a team of researchers and professionals skilled in investment strategy, such as CFAs or Chartered Financial Analysts. They select the investments, monitor them and decide when they should be sold. Typically, they require their clients to have a minimum net worth beforehand, usually starting at $1,000,000 excluding the equity in your home. They normally charge fees based on the amount of assets they are managing for you and these fees can range from 0.25% to 2% or more. The more assets they manage for you, the lower the fees. What you're paying for is personal service, an individualized portfolio that meets your specific goals and objectives and ongoing monitoring and management of your money.

As in all businesses, there are good advisors and not-so-good advisors. We're all still reeling from the story of Bernie Madoff and wondering how we can protect ourselves from con-men like him. References are good but let's face it, no-one is going to tell you to talk to someone that would have a negative opinion. And professional certifications and advanced degrees are not a guarantee of credibility. Even Bernie Madoff was registered with the SEC – in fact, he even headed up NASDAQ at one time. I don't know how one can be assured that they'll never encounter a dishonest money-manager. I can only tell you that it's important to ask questions and understand what your advisor is doing with your money. Trust your instincts and if it sounds too good to be true, it probably isn't true. Today, if someone promises you more than about five percent on your portfolio with no risk or uses the word "guarantee", be very wary or just head in the opposite direction.

Robo-Advisors

For investors who don't have the minimum net worth requirements for professional managers and don't want to be actively involved in the management of their portfolio, there are Robo-Advisors. Robo Advisors provide investment management online, based on algorithms, with minimal human intervention. So basically a computer is managing your money for you. This isn't such a bad thing, really. There have been many studies that have shown index funds have outperformed active money managers over the years. Index funds are computer generated funds that mimic exactly the securities in the underlying index.

The reason for the increasing popularity of Robo-Advisors is that you don't need to have a minimum amount of net worth to participate. Younger investors, in particular, like them because they are so used to doing almost everything online. You don't have to be wealthy, or hire an expensive advisor to invest your money. Robo-Advisors have the technology to create an asset allocation strategy for you, based on your personal needs and goals, at an affordable price. But while robo-advisors do provide a service, it's the financial advisors who provide the experience and can help you navigate through the market highs and lows without losing sight of your financial goals. They can help facilitate the decisions required through various life phases to determine what is most important in your life.

Having said that, there are a number of Robo-Advisors out there that you may want to investigate, including:

Betterment - www.betterment.com
Wealthfront – www.wealthfront.com
Personal Capital – www.personalcapital.com
Stash – www.stashinvest.com
WiseBanyan – www.wisebanyan.com
SigFig – www.sigfig.com
Vanguard and Charles Schwab also offer robo-advisory services

LearnVest (www.learnvest.com) is a firm started by a woman named Alexa Von Tobel in 2009. She was a trader at Morgan Stanley and became concerned that many employees were now responsible for their own retirement income but had little training or experience in managing those funds. She was able to raise over $70 million of financing to start one of the first robo-advisors. In 2015, Learnvest was acquired by Northwestern Mutual Capital.

Just recently, Sallie Krawcheck, the former President of the Global Wealth and Investment Management division of Bank of America, founded Ellevest (www.ellevest.com), a robo-advisor created specifically for women. It should be up and running this year, 2016, and is definitely worth checking into because their mission is to empower women financially. Sound familiar?

Once you have your investment plan in place, monitor it regularly and make changes when necessary but try not to be tempted to time the market because no one has ever done it successfully, all the time. In any given year, the market can experience a big move, such as what we witnessed in 2008 when the market declined by about thirty-seven percent. It was scary that year, there is no doubt. Many people panicked and sold everything, thus locking in some pretty big losses. They then lost all confidence in the stock market and didn't reinvest the money. In 2009, the market was up twenty-seven percent and over the next six years, it continued to go up at an average annual rate of thirteen percent. If you were a long-term investor in 2008 and stayed invested, you would have not only recovered any paper loss from 2008, but you would have a highly appreciated portfolio today. As we all know, nothing goes up forever just as nothing stays down forever.

Over the last seventy-five years or so, the average annual return of the stock market has been about seven percent. There is a mathematical formula called the "Rule of 72." If you divide the return you are getting into 72, you can calculate the number of years it will take for you to double your money. So if you're getting an average annual return of seven percent, you'll double your money every ten years. Investing in stocks or stock funds shouldn't intimidate you or be considered "gambling" if you have a good plan. As we mentioned earlier, if you need your money within one to three years, then limit your stock investments and invest most of your money in short-term bonds or cash and cash equivalents. But if you have a longer-term time horizon, the stock market will give you the better return and that is the way you will grow your wealth. Forgive me for repeating myself but it's such an important concept. As you get closer to retirement, the asset mix allocation in your retirement portfolios should be moving more into bonds or fixed income mutual funds with a decreasing percentage in stocks or stock mutual funds.

If you have an advisor or someone managing your money, make sure you understand what they are doing. Ask the following questions before agreeing to an investment suggestion and whenever you meet for a review of your investment portfolio.

- On a scale of 1 to 10, what is the risk level of my portfolio? (10 is the riskiest)
- What sort of return can I expect from this portfolio/ investment?
- Is this a tax efficient portfolio?
- Do I have a certain percentage in cash or cash equivalents in case I need some funds?
- What are the fees that I'm paying?

Try to avoid making these mistakes when putting together your investment strategy:

- Expect to find high returns with low risk
- Make an investment decision without considering the tax implications

- Take undue risk in one area and avoid rational risk in another
- Not diversifying by "putting all your eggs in the same basket"
- Copy the behavior of others even in the face of unfavorable outcomes
- React to external news without considering the impact to your personal goals
- Be too optimistic; i.e. "bad things only happen to other people"
- Buy high and sell low

And most importantly, don't panic and don't get greedy. Don't let emotions drive your decisions about money. Emotional decisions, whether you panic and sell when the market is going down or buying "just because everyone else is", are an investor's worst enemy. If you plan to manage your own investments, be sure you have the temperament to do so. Tune out the headlines and don't worry if you made a bad decision. Most of us have made bad decisions in our lives and that's ok. Hopefully, we learn from each mistake. I advise my clients to grit their teeth and sell an investment when it needs to be sold rather than waiting for it to come back to the original purchase price. First of all, those funds can be placed elsewhere with prospects for a better return and even more importantly, you're not reminded of that "mistake" each time you open your investment statement. Set a long-term goal, diversify your investments and stay the course. One of my priorities as a financial planner is to help my clients stay the course, not panic and focus primarily on their goals and objectives. Sometimes doing nothing is the best strategy.

Chapter 5
Plan to Retire Comfortably

Planning for retirement involves many decisions, particularly if you are between the ages of fifty-five and seventy. These include:

- How and when do I start to take Social Security benefits?
- Medicare might not cover everything, so what type of supplemental medical insurance do I need?
- Do I need to buy long-term care insurance? Or disability insurance?
- How much can I withdraw from my retirement account every year to maintain my standard of living?
- Will I run out of money?
- What amount do I need to have saved by the time I retire?
- If I need to continue working longer than I expected, do I need to update my work skills?

New trends in our society are changing the way people work, live and spend money. Today, the average American will probably not retire until age seventy-five and it has become increasingly common to be over sixty-five and working. Some of us choose to work longer while others of us have no choice but to continue working to pay the bills. Also, longer lives can mean longer careers or working part-time during your retirement years. As women, the odds of living into our eighties and nineties are high, so we need to plan carefully to make sure we don't outlive our money. One of the most important components of a good financial plan is a retirement strategy that ensures that won't happen. It's usually not too late to start planning, but so much easier when you begin at an early age.

We all know we need a good retirement plan and a good estate plan in order to protect the assets we've accumulated, live a comfortable life and pass whatever is left to our heirs or donate them to a favorite charity, if we choose. But it never ceases to surprise me how few people actually do have a good plan. I can understand how young people roll their eyes when one mentions retirement. When you're young and starting your career, retirement has no reality. And I recognize that people with low incomes find it very difficult to make ends meet, let alone put money aside for retirement. But if you can find it within your budget to save some of your income, then by all means do it. Many people fail to prepare adequately for their retirement years because they tend to their current needs first at the expense of their long-term goals. As we grow older and approach retirement, we want to make sure we have enough money to live in the lifestyle we choose and not run out before we die. You may or may not want to leave anything for beneficiaries but you'll need to take care of yourself.

Until about 1980 or so, most companies in the U.S. provided their employees with a pension or a "defined benefit" retirement plan. Pensions mean that the company you work for promises you certain benefits down the road. You work for the company for a number of years and receive a pre-determined pension when you retire. Oh, if that were only the case for all of us today. But unfortunately, today just twenty-five percent of people in the workforce have pensions. Pensions are great because the responsibility of managing those funds is placed on the company, not the employee. Today most employees have "defined contribution" retirement plans at work where the responsibility of investing the money is placed on the employee, not the employer.

401(k) and 403(b) Plans

In the early 1980's, there was a shift from defined benefit plans to "defined contribution" plans. We know them more commonly as 401(k) or 403(b) plans, although there are a number of other defined contribution plans as well such as SEP IRAs, ESOPs and various others that one could write volumes on just that subject. 403(b) plans are also called 457 plans. A defined contribution plan does not promise a specific amount of benefits at retirement – rather it's dependent on how the funds perform in the retirement plan. The responsibility for making investment decisions is on you, the participant, and if you are successful in achieving good returns, you will have the income necessary to retire comfortably. The average person has little experience or knowledge about investing and yet they are solely responsible for making sure their retirement funds are invested well. If you are not very experienced in investing, I would strongly advise you to become more financially literate or hire an advisor for help. There is good information on the internet and community colleges offer basic investing courses for adults as well. This is the money you will need to live on when you retire and as we are living longer, the money has to last longer. Since Social Security was never meant to fund our retirement completely and company pensions are not common anymore, we'll have to make a plan and ensure that we invest our money wisely.

A participant in a defined contribution plan has a certain percentage of their income deducted from their paycheck each time they are paid and it's deducted on a pre-tax basis. Sometimes the employer makes contributions as well. They might 'match' the participant's contribution, up to a certain percentage limit, or they might make a discretionary profit-sharing distribution if business has been good and they choose to share the wealth with their employees. Most plans offer a number of mutual funds from which the participant must choose and the money is then allocated to those funds. The investments grow tax-deferred, meaning you don't pay tax on the gains made each year, and are available for your use when you retire. You do pay tax once you begin to withdraw the money.

401(k) plans and 403(b) plans are very similar except that the former is usually offered by private companies and the latter by federal, state and local government entities and non-profit organizations. Annual contribution limits are increased most years – in 2016, the limit for workers under the age of fifty is $18,000 and for those over fifty, it's $24,000. This doesn't include an employer's matching contributions. If your employer offers a "match" or "profit-sharing" contribution, the total combined contributions are capped at $53,000 for workers under 50 and $59,000 for those over 50. Combined contributions include the employee's and employer's contributions. In order to make the most of your employer's contribution, you should be contributing an amount that is enough to qualify for the full match. I would strongly advise that if your employer does offer a match, then do whatever you can to defer the minimum amount needed to meet that match. After all, it's 'free' money. If you aren't sure about the amount you should be contributing, seek advice from a financial advisor or your human resources department.

Individual Retirement Accounts (IRAs)

If you don't have access to a company sponsored retirement plan but you have earned income, you can start an Individual Retirement Account, better known as an IRA. You can contribute to an IRA at any age so for those of you with children who have part-time or summer jobs, you might want to talk to them about saving part of their earnings in an IRA. The sooner one starts to save, the more money one will have at retirement. I talk to young people and tell them that if they started an IRA at age 21, contributed $5,500 every year for 44 years, and invested the funds in an S&P 500 Index mutual fund with an average annual return of 7%, they would have $1,571,621 by the time they are 65 years old. And that is just in their IRA. Hopefully, they'll have other company sponsored retirement plans that will add to their retirement funds. IRAs are a very common way to grow your retirement savings and they are easy to set up.

Even if you have access to and are participating in a retirement plan at work, you can still have an IRA account, but the contribution would not be tax-deductible. The downside of IRAs, however, is the maximum contribution amounts are much lower than 401(k) or 403(b) plans. In 2016, IRA contributions cannot exceed $5,500 or $6,500 for those over 50. If you are a non-working spouse, you can open a spousal IRA and make contributions in the same amounts as regular IRAs. I would encourage any non-working spouse who is reading this and has not already done so, to open a Spousal IRA.

In addition to income tax, there is usually a 10% charge if you take money out of your IRA before age 59 ½, which is called an early or premature withdrawal penalty tax. There are exceptions to this rule and they include the following:

- Medical expenses for you, your spouse & dependents

- First time purchase of your principal residence (also includes home purchases for those who haven't owned a home in more than five years).

- Tuition & educational expenses (including room & board) for you, your spouse and dependents

- Prevention of eviction or foreclosure on your principal residence

- Funeral or burial expenses for family members & dependents

- Damages to your principal residence in excess of 10% of your adjusted gross income (AGI)

401(k) and 403(b) plans have early withdrawal penalties as well as exceptions similar to IRAs.

However, one of the main differences between the two types of retirement plans is that you can borrow from your 401(k) or 403(b) plan. If your plan does offer a loan provision, you can only borrow from the balance accumulated and vested in your account. Loans are limited to fifty-percent of your account balance or a maximum of $50,000, whichever is less, and are generally required to be paid back with interest and within five years. But keep in mind that you're paying the interest to yourself. If you leave the company, you must pay back the loan in full.

Roth IRAs

A Roth IRA differs from a traditional IRA in that the contributions you make are with income that has already been taxed so you normally won't pay tax when you take the money out, if you have held the IRA for at least five years. That is to say, if you only withdraw what you originally put in and not any of the earnings, then you won't be taxed. The contribution limits are the same as for a regular IRA. Roth IRAs make the most sense if you expect to have higher tax rates after you retire than what you have presently. There is a common misperception that our tax rates will be lower after we retire, but that's not necessarily the case for everyone. Many retirees still have income in the form of pensions, rental income, consulting fees and such, that puts them in an equal or possibly higher tax bracket than when they were working. So a Roth IRA can end up being a great investment vehicle to minimize your tax liabilities over a long period of time after you retire.

Taking a distribution from your Roth IRA before age 59 ½ and before holding the IRA for at least five years, will also incur the ten percent penalty, but the same exceptions apply as mentioned above for a regular IRA. In addition to the penalties for early withdrawal, there are some eligibility requirements for Roth IRAs that you need to keep in mind. For the 2016 tax year, you cannot contribute to a Roth IRA if you're single and your adjusted gross income (AGI) is greater than $132,000. For married couples filing jointly, that amount is $194,000. And just to confuse us further, the IRS has said that we can make a partial contribution to a Roth IRA if our income falls between $117,000 and $132,000 for single persons or between $184,000 and $194,000 for married persons, filing jointly. Check with your financial advisor or tax-preparer if you're not sure whether you qualify for a Roth IRA.

Rollover IRAs

What do you do with your 401(k) or 403(b) plan if you change jobs? Basically, you have three choices:

- Leave it at your former company, if they will allow it
- Move the funds to your new company's plan, if they offer one that allows it
- Roll it over into an IRA

There are advantages and disadvantages to each of these choices and the decision depends on what is most appropriate for your situation. My preference would be for you to open a Rollover IRA and move the funds into that vehicle so that you can direct and manage the account yourself. But for those of you who don't want that responsibility, then keeping it in your old plan or moving it to a new company-sponsored plan would be the best choice. The important thing to keep in mind is that you don't want to cash out and receive the funds outright because you'll incur tax consequences and possibly penalties, as well.

Annuities

An annuity is a financial product typically sold through insurance companies, brokers and banks that are designed to pay out a stream of payments to an individual for a certain period or for the rest of their life, in exchange for a lump sum of cash. "Immediate annuities" pay the income now while "deferred annuities" pay the income at some point in the future. There are basically two types of annuities; fixed and variable.

1. Fixed annuities – the amount of monthly payments is pre-determined and will remain the same for the rest of your life. Fixed annuities are much more attractive in high interest rate environments because the underlying investments are in bonds, or fixed income securities. High interest rates on bonds will provide a higher income stream.

2. Variable annuities – the funds are invested in the equity markets and therefore, the amount of monthly payments will depend on the performance of the underlying investments. The owner of the annuity takes on the risk of investing in the stock market – when the market is up, the monthly payments will be higher than when the market is down.

Be sure you understand the reason you're purchasing an annuity and what fees are involved. Annuities have very high, upfront sales charges and most have surrender penalty fees if you decide to cash out and take your money within a certain time period, normally seven years. They should be purchased only if they complement your entire financial plan because they are usually pretty complex and difficult to understand. They aren't for everyone. If you are eligible to receive Social Security or if you have a pension from your employer, you already have an annuity that will pay you a fixed amount for the rest of your life. I would suggest you seek the advice of an objective professional (not the one selling you the annuity) before making the investment. Your CPA or a fee-only financial planner can give you that objective advice.

Social Security

Social Security is important to every retiree and it's important to know that there are a number of strategies one can use to claim benefits. In the U.S., it's known as the Old Age, Survivors and Disability Federal Insurance Program, better known by the acronym OASDI. The original law was enacted in 1935 by President Franklin Roosevelt to benefit mostly lower paid workers to ensure they didn't have to retire in complete poverty. The Social Security Administration (SSA) and the Internal Revenue Service (IRS) keep track of your earnings and will determine the benefits available to you at your retirement. The amount you will receive depends on how much you earned during your working years and at what age you choose to retire and claim those benefits. Social Security was never meant to fund one's retirement entirely but it does ensure a consistent and increasing income stream.

The SSA and IRS also determine your full retirement age (FRA), the age at which you can claim your full benefits and this has been increasing in recent years. For example, if you were born in 1960 or later, your full retirement age will be sixty-seven. The earliest you can start to receive benefits is age sixty-two, but you will receive substantially less (about thirty percent less) than if you waited until your full retirement age. Conversely, if you are in a financial position to wait until age seventy (the latest you can start collecting), your benefits will rise about eight percent per year after your full retirement age. Waiting is not always the right choice for everyone. Each option should be evaluated, taking into account your own personal circumstances. So it's very important to determine the most optimum time for you to start collecting your social security benefits. I suggest that you go to the website www.SSA.gov and check to see what your full retirement age is and what your benefits would be then and at age seventy. Very wealthy people may not care whether they receive a Social Security check or not, but for the not-so-very wealthy, that monthly benefit will make up, on average, about twenty-five to thirty percent of one's retirement income. If you have earned income and receive a W-2 form, you can calculate how much is deducted from your paycheck each month for Social Security. It's a tax called FICA, or the Federal Insurance Contributions Act. With few exceptions, all salaried income has a FICA tax on it – that's how our Social Security program is funded. Remember, Social Security funds are your money that is saved for you by the government.

There are a variety of options one can choose for how and when to begin receiving benefits and each has its' own benefits and drawbacks. This is where a good financial planner can be of great help to determine the best age to start taking benefits and what the advantages or disadvantages would be in your situation. If you continue to work after receiving Social Security benefits, you will be taxed on earnings over a certain amount, so that has to be taken into consideration as well. But the benefits are indexed to inflation and usually increase each year, so they are a very important part of your retirement income stream. Your financial planner will know your specific situation, your goals and your retirement objectives and can help you make the most appropriate decisions regarding your Social Security benefits.

Married couples should apply a joint optimization strategy when they are making plans on when to take Social Security benefits. As a general rule, it makes sense for the higher earner to delay taking benefits. The lower earner can take benefits at their full retirement age, then when the higher earner starts to take benefits at age seventy, the lower earner spouse can switch and take half of the higher earners benefits.

Divorced women are eligible for a benefit equal to one-half of the amount their ex-spouse would receive at his/her full retirement age as long as they start receiving benefits at their full retirement age. This is called the Divorced Spousal Benefit. The marriage must have lasted ten years or longer and the divorced spouse must not be married at the time of claiming the benefit. If the divorced spouse's benefit is larger than one-half of her ex-spouses' benefit, then it obviously makes more sense to claim her own benefit. But if it's less, then she should claim the Divorced Spousal Benefit, if possible.

So when is the best time to start taking Social Security benefits? Unfortunately, there's no "one-size-fits-all" answer. If you need the money to pay your monthly expenses, then of course you will start your benefits as soon as you can get them. If you don't need the money right away, the decision is harder. My advice to my clients is to try to wait as long as possible to take Social Security benefits or at least until your full retirement age. If you're still working at your full retirement age or have other retirement funds to use, it might make more sense to wait until age seventy to collect your Social Security benefits. Where else can you get a guaranteed eight percent return on your money? By taking steps as early as possible to have a retirement fund, you'll be in a much better position to choose when to retire and to take advantage of a higher Social Security benefit for the rest of your life. Seek the help of the Social Security office or a financial advisor to plan a strategy that works best for you.

Medicare

Health care costs are probably the biggest deterrent to a secure and financially stable retirement. Unfortunately, many young people aren't thinking about, much less planning for, health care costs in retirement. And as we get older, too many of us assume that our employers will continue to pay for our health care premiums after we turn sixty-five. The fact is that fewer and fewer companies are offering health care to people over the age of sixty-five who qualify for Medicare. Only one in five companies with five hundred or more employees, offers health insurance to Medicare-eligible employees. So if you're still working past the age of sixty-five, the only health care coverage you're likely to have is Medicare. It's important that you understand exactly what Medicare is all about and what benefits it provides. Because health care costs continue to rise, paying for health care should now be taken into even greater consideration when planning for retirement.

Medicare provides health coverage to about fifty million people aged sixty-five or older or those who are disabled. As soon as you turn sixty-five years old, you are eligible to sign up for Medicare Part A and Part B, but be aware that you may have to pay premiums for Part B. Part A covers hospital stays, skilled nursing, home health care and hospice. A benefit period begins on the first day you start to receive the services and ends after sixty consecutive days for each benefit period. There is no limit to the number of benefit periods for each individual. The services not included are custodial care services which includes a nursing care facility that provides assistance with activities of daily living, such as eating, bathing and dressing.

If you have Part A coverage you can elect Part B coverage as well but you have to sign up for it during the open enrollment period, otherwise there might be a penalty fee if you sign up later. The services for Part B include doctor's visits, ambulance transportation, diagnostic tests, outpatient therapy and home health care. Part B does not cover dental care, cosmetic surgery, hearing aids or eye exams. I couldn't believe the cost of hearing aids when we ordered them for my mother – about $5,000 - and that was seven years ago.

While Medicare is a decent system, it only covers about sixty percent of health care costs. It does cover preventive care, but you will still have to pay premiums, co-pays, deductibles and co-insurance unless you have some sort of supplemental coverage. AARP advises that if you call your doctor for your annual check-up, you need to ask for a "wellness" assessment, not a check-up. Every Medicare participant receives a free "wellness" assessment once a year, but a "check-up" might incur a co-payment or other costs. If you're single and earn more than $85,000, or if you're a couple with joint income of more than $170,000, you can expect to pay higher premiums as well.

In addition, Medicare doesn't normally cover medical expenses incurred when you're travelling outside the U.S. The good news is that, as women, we generally take better care of our health than men. We tend to have regular check-ups and will see a doctor when a problem occurs. The message here is to take good care of yourself so that you can keep your medical expenses to a minimum. A good diet, regular exercise and reduction of stress are the key ingredients to staying healthy as we age.

I will only touch briefly on Medicaid here because my wish for all of you reading this book is that you will never need it. Medicaid is a joint federal and state social welfare program that provides health care to families and individuals with limited resources. It's a wonderful safety net for those that need it, but in order to qualify one has to have essentially no assets. Some states allow an individual to keep their home. We've all heard the stories of families retitling assets from an elderly person's name, so that he or she could qualify for Medicaid and the family wouldn't be burdened with high medical expenses. But today, the government looks back five years, so if you moved assets within that time, your family member would not qualify for the program. But as I said, I hope you never have to consider Medicaid for your health care needs.

In summary, think about the following as you plan for your retirement:

1. First and foremost, decide when you want to retire and where you'd like to retire.

2. Decide on how much you need to live the life you'd like in retirement.

3. Figure out where the money will come from; savings, retirement accounts, social security, pensions or annuities.

4. Calculate how much you will need to save today to have the funds needed when you retire.

5. And finally, set realistic goals.

Chapter 6
Protect Your Assets

Discussing death, disability or destruction of personal property is hardly anyone's favorite topic of conversation. But unfortunately, "stuff" happens and we need to protect, preserve and plan for as much as possible. Managing that risk with insurance is an essential part of financial planning because protecting your assets, your property and your health is a top priority. Rather than take on the risk yourself and possibly lose assets when an "event" occurs, you transfer that risk to an insurance company and in exchange, you pay them a premium. If a loss occurs, your assets are protected and the insurance company will "make you whole" again.

Health Insurance

Let's start with health insurance because I'm sure we would all agree that maintaining good health is a top priority. We also all know how expensive health care is today and the costs just seem to be increasing all the time. If you are fortunate to be covered by your employer's group health plan, you should take full advantage of it. Employers used to pay the full premiums but now pay a lesser share, pushing more of the burden on the employee. If you are leaving your employer either by your choice or a normal termination, you will be entitled to COBRA for a specific period of time. COBRA is an acronym for the "Consolidated Omnibus Budget Reconciliation Act", which Congress passed in 1986. The law contains provisions that give certain former employees, retirees, spouses and dependent children the right to continue their health coverage at the employer's group rates. Group rate premiums are always lower than individual rate premiums. Normally, COBRA is offered for eighteen months after termination of employment, but if the employee died or was divorced, the family receives the benefits for thirty-six months.

Health care plans these days offer an array of choices which sometimes can be very confusing. HMOs, PPOs, High Deductibles, etc. – how does one choose the best plan? An HMO is a Health Maintenance Organization and a PPO is a Preferred Provider Organization. The difference between the two is that you have a choice of physicians with a PPO, while with an HMO you have to have a primary physician within that provider network who will then refer you to specialists when needed.

Normally, with an HMO, your health costs will only be covered if you see a doctor within that network. That is why HMO's often have lower monthly premiums and out-of-pocket costs. PPO's give you much more flexibility when choosing a doctor or a hospital. They also have a network of providers but there are fewer restrictions if you choose to see a doctor out of their network. Premiums tend to be higher and there is usually a deductible and a co-payment. If you have a choice between these two types of plans, consider your specific medical needs and the premiums you can afford. If you have health issues and don't want to change doctors, then a PPO would be more appropriate. But if you're considering an HMO, take a close look at the network to determine if the choices of doctors and medical facilities will meet your needs.

Most PPO health policies have deductibles and co-payments. A deductible is a fixed amount that you pay each year before the insurance kicks in and covers the rest of your costs. For example, if you have a $2000 deductible, then you'll pay one hundred percent of your medical bills until you reach $2000. After that, the insurance company will pay the bills for the rest of the year. Usually higher deductible policies have lower monthly premiums. A co-payment is a fixed amount that you might have to pay each time you receive a medical service. The deductible and the co-payment amounts are both fixed amounts, which means that they don't change based on the amount of your medical bill.

HSAs – Health Savings Accounts

If you choose to enroll in a high-deductible insurance plan and you're under age sixty-five, you might want to consider starting a Health Savings Accounts, or an HSA. Your employer might offer an HSA or you can start one at a bank or brokerage firm. Basically, you are putting money aside that is not taxed and can be used to pay for medical expenses not covered by your insurance. It can also be used to pay the deductibles and co-payments. If you're generally healthy and want to save for healthcare costs or if you're near retirement, then an HSA makes sense. On the other hand, if you have health issues requiring frequent medical services and you would find it hard to meet a high deductible, then an HSA is not your best option. A word of caution: if you take money out of your HSA to pay for non-medical expenses, you'll have to pay taxes on it.

Long-Term Care Insurance

Long term care is generally defined as assistance provided for an extended period of time for people who can't care for themselves because of illness, cognitive impairment like Alzheimer's or dementia or a prolonged disability. It covers care normally not provided by health insurance, Medicare or Medicaid. This would include home care, assisted living, adult day care and nursing homes. Most policies require that a physician certify that you can't perform at least two activities of daily living, such as eating, bathing or dressing, on your own.

The best time to buy long-term care insurance is when you're in your fifties. It starts getting more difficult and expensive by age sixty and becomes cost-prohibitive by age seventy. According to AARP (American Association of Retired Persons), the average cost of a private room in a nursing home today is over $90,000 per year and in-home health care averages over $45,000 per year, depending on the level of care needed. Premiums used to be the same for both men and women, but recently they have been increasing for women because it's more likely that we will live longer.

There are many types of long-term care insurance and describing the details of each type is beyond the scope of this book. I would suggest that you seek the help of a reputable insurance broker who can find a policy to meet your specific needs. My advice to clients who are about twenty years or more from retirement and can afford it, is to think about self-insuring for their long-term care needs. A diversified investment portfolio, compounded over twenty years, should yield the funds necessary to cover the average cost of a skilled long-term care facility or in-home care. You might even want to keep these funds in a separate account designated specifically for your long-term care needs.

Disability Insurance

If you are a one-income household with dependent children, disability insurance is as important as life insurance. We have a much greater chance of becoming disabled than dying at an early age. The odds increase if the work you do involves more physical exertion. Caregivers, for example, are particularly vulnerable to back injuries. But white collar workers can suffer an accident or illness that causes an extended absence from work. Even if both you and your spouse work, the loss of fifty percent of the household income can be devastating. Like long-term care insurance, if you have the ability to self-insure, that would be great. But if not, try to avoid tapping into your retirement funds to replace temporary lost income unless you have no other choice. Buying a disability insurance policy would replace part or all of that lost income.

Many large employers still provide disability insurance and pay for the premiums. But an increasing number of employers are lowering the amount of insurance while giving employees the option to purchase more with their own money through a payroll deduction. But, no surprise, most people don't purchase more when they have this option. There are so many choices and it can become so confusing so we put it off or think we don't need it. Maybe we have our six-month emergency funds, or we can tap into our retirement accounts or perhaps we have relatives that will help out. It doesn't really matter what type of work you do if an illness or accident causes you to be away from that work for an extended period of time without income. Think of disability insurance as "income-replacement" insurance because that's what it's intended to do. It's an essential part of your financial plan whether you are single or have a family - someone has to take care of you and pay the bills while you're sick or disabled.

Most employers will cover short-term disability because the premiums are less and generally, most of us can survive financially with a short illness or accident. But long-term disability is the issue and consider yourselves very lucky if your employer offers this coverage and pays for the premiums, as well. Usually long-term coverage replaces up to two thirds of your income if you can't do your job or any job, depending on the terms of the policy.

Private insurance does offer a more expansive definition of disability. Know the difference between "own occupation" and "any occupation." The former means you cannot perform your own work, while the latter means you can't work at any job. "Any occupation" is more expensive, naturally, and more in line with Social Security disability requirements. It's important to look at the terms and see exactly what is covered and when the insurance payments will start. The disability coverage offered by Social Security helps a bit, but it requires a strict definition of disability and can sometimes take time to collect the benefits. An advantage of private insurance is that it may replace a greater part of your income than Social Security would. Social Security benefits are based on your average lifetime earnings and can't exceed $2,639 per month for 2016.

Any disability benefit you receive is taxable if your employer pays for your premiums, and tax-free if you buy the insurance on your own. If you are a self-employed person, you have the choice to deduct the premiums as a business expense, in which case any payouts would be taxable, or you can pay for the premiums with after-tax money, in which case any payouts would not be taxable. This matters, so check with your financial planner or tax-preparer before you choose which way is best for you.

Homeowner's Insurance

Most people who own a home have homeowner's insurance because it's required by our mortgage lender. Even if you don't have a mortgage or have paid it off, you need to have insurance protection. In general, homeowner's insurance covers damage to your home caused by fire, theft and certain natural disasters. Depending on where you live, you may need to purchase additional coverage for protection from earthquakes or floods as these potentially devastating events are not covered in most basic policies. But we all need the insurance because it will save us thousands, maybe even millions, of dollars if our home is damaged or destroyed.

Most homeowner's policies have a deductible and are based on a replacement cost of the house and adjoining structures. Insurance companies let you choose your deductible (usually $500 or $1000) but the replacement cost is based on their appraisal of your home. The important thing to remember with your policy is to adjust the replacement cost as needed. Building materials and costs continue to rise every year, so it might be much more expensive to repair or rebuild your home now than when it was first purchased. And if you increased the size of your home, added a structure or made significant improvements, make sure to inform your insurance company and increase the replacement cost. A good rule of thumb is to review your policy on an annual basis for these very reasons.

A home warranty is not a substitute for homeowner's insurance although it's good to have and many realtors include at least one year of home warranty insurance as a closing gift to their clients when they purchase a new home. Home warranties cover damage to appliances such as refrigerators or water heaters, plus some physical parts of your home. But they don't cover losses or damage due to theft or natural events – those would be covered by your homeowner's insurance. If you can afford both homeowner's insurance and a home warranty, that would be the way to go, but if you can only afford one, then it would have to be homeowner's insurance.

Along with your homeowner's insurance, you should also consider buying an umbrella policy for coverage of at least $1,000,000. It's not expensive at all, as a $1,000,000 policy will probably cost about $200 per year. It's considered extra liability insurance as it provides coverage above the limits of your homeowner's insurance and it's designed to help protect you from any lawsuits or claims against your assets. Here's how an umbrella policy works. Let's say you're involved in a car accident and you're at fault. The driver of the other car is injured and your automobile insurance only covers him up to $250,000 for his injuries. This sounds like a lot of coverage but imagine if the driver of the car was a surgeon and, because of his injuries, he can't perform surgery for a few months. So he sues you for $1,000,000 to cover his lost income. Your personal umbrella policy will then step in to cover any damages over and above the coverage of your automobile insurance. Believe me, it's a small price to pay for peace of mind.

Personal Property Insurance

When I work with my clients to prepare a statement of their net worth, they sometimes forget to mention all the valuable personal property they own. Everyone lists their real-estate, cars and boats, but what about jewelry, artwork or antiques and other collectibles in your home? These are items that are likely increasing in value each year and probably worth much more than you think. Most homeowners' insurance policies will cover the contents of your home up to a certain limit. But if you have specific items of great value, you should get an appraisal and insure them separately in what is called Scheduled Personal Property insurance. That way, if they are damaged, lost or stolen, the insurance will cover the cost of replacement. Remember not only to send your insurer a detailed description of the asset, but also several photos of each item.

Life Insurance

To buy or not to buy? That is frequently the question I get from my clients. My answer is always based on who will suffer financial hardship in the event of your death. Certainly, if you have young children, you should have life insurance. Many employers offer life insurance as a benefit but only up to a certain amount. So should you buy additional coverage and for how much? The reason most of us hesitate is that the premiums can be high but they only increase as we get older, so the sooner you decide, the better. Plus, none of us wants to think that we will die prematurely, but as I said earlier, "stuff happens."

There are basically two types of life insurance – whole life and term. If you talk to an insurance broker, you'll find that there are many, many variations on these two basic types of insurance. I don't have the expertise to go into all the different types of life insurance policies and strategies, so I would suggest that you speak to a licensed and reputable insurance broker when you're ready. But decide first if you need whole life or term insurance. Here are the differences:

- Whole Life covers you throughout your life and ends only on your death while term is for a specific period of time, like ten or twenty years.

- Whole life has an investment component added in so that you build up a cash value over the years. Part of the premium you pay is invested for you and the cash value becomes an asset that you can use if necessary. However, beware of the built-in fees and surrender charges that can eat up much of that cash value.

- Term insurance has fixed premiums that are paid monthly for the term of the policy. If you should die during that term, death benefits are paid to your beneficiaries.

- In both whole life and term policies, the death benefits are not taxable to the beneficiary.

- Whole life is used frequently for very large estates. The death benefit presumably will cover any estate tax due so that the beneficiaries are not obligated to sell assets to pay the taxes.

- Whole life is also better if you have a child with special needs and will be financially dependent on you their whole lives. They will need to have that financial security after your death as well, so permanent coverage is better.

- Term insurance can be used in many ways, but most commonly to cover household and college expenses if a parent dies prematurely or to cover mortgage payments if a spouse dies before the mortgage is paid off. So you can match the length of the term period to your anticipated period of need.

- Premiums for whole life insurance are about ten times higher than that of term insurance.

- Whole life insurance pays higher commissions to brokers than term insurance, so keep that in mind if someone is trying to sell you a whole life policy when term insurance would be adequate to meet your needs.

Reverse Mortgages

As more and more baby boomers are entering their retirement years, we are witnessing an upsurge in the use of reverse mortgages. We've certainly seen more celebrities advertising reverse mortgages on television, so what are they exactly?

For the average American, the largest part of their net worth is the equity in their home. This equity can be tapped to supplement retirement income, pay off a mortgage or cover healthcare expenses, should you need it. You can either sell your home and downsize to a smaller or less expensive one, take out a home equity line of credit or consider a reverse mortgage when you need to supplement your income. If you are sixty-two years of age or older, a reverse mortgage allows you to convert part of the equity in your home into cash without having to sell your home. But I caution you to look very closely at the details in a reverse mortgage document and even better yet, get some professional advice before signing.

With a regular, conventional mortgage, you make payments to a lender every month in order to own your home after a certain period of time. With a reverse mortgage, you receive money from the lender. Part of the equity in your home is taken and converted into monthly payments to you, usually on a tax-free basis. It also shouldn't affect your Social Security or Medicare payments. Generally, you don't have to pay the money back for as long as you live in the house. When you die, sell the house or move out, your spouse or beneficiaries have to repay the loan.

A big mistake that people make when taking out a reverse mortgage is that they don't include their spouse on the loan. So when the borrower dies, the surviving spouse is forced to pay back the loan and sometimes this means the house must be sold. In some instances, a non-borrowing spouse may be able to remain in the house but will probably not receive any payments. Reverse mortgage loans are not the same, but the following are some issues to consider before taking out the loan:

1. Increasing Balance – your loan gets bigger over time as opposed to a regular mortgage that decreases over time. As you receive the monthly payments from your lender, interest is added on to the balance of the loan. This means that the amount you owe grows as the interest adds up over time.

2. Variable Rates – Most reverse mortgage loans have variable rates that are tied to a financial index and may change over time as market rates change. Some reverse mortgages offer fixed rates but they tend to require you to take the loan as a lump sum at closing.

3. Fees and closing costs – Reverse mortgage lenders generally charge an origination fee and other closing costs as well as servicing fees over the life of the loan. Some lenders also require you to purchase mortgage insurance.

4. Tax-deductibility – the interest on a reverse mortgage loan is **not** tax-deductible each year on your tax returns. If you pay off the loan partially or in full, you may be able

to deduct part of the interest paid, but check with your tax preparer or advisor beforehand.

5. Property taxes and maintenance – In a reverse mortgage, you keep the title to your home, so you're responsible for property taxes, insurance, maintenance and utility expenses. If property taxes and other expenses aren't paid, the lender may require you to repay the loan. A financial assessment is required when you apply for the mortgage and the lender might reduce your monthly payments as a "set-aside" amount to ensure that property tax and insurance payments are met.

6. Your heirs – Reverse mortgages frequently use up all or most of the equity in your home which means less for your heirs. Most reverse mortgages have a "non-recourse" clause stating that you, or your estate, cannot owe more than the value of your home when the loan becomes due and the home is sold. However, if you or your heirs want to pay off the loan and keep the home, rather than selling it, you wouldn't have to pay more than the appraised value.

Chapter 7
Everyone Needs an Estate Plan

Securing your family's future with an inheritance is a wonderful testament to a life of hard work and love. Leaving a legacy for your children, grandchildren, or the causes you love is an important objective for many of us. This area of financial planning involves getting expert legal advice in addition to working with a qualified financial professional. But the reality of the situation today is that most people don't think that they need an estate plan or they put it off until it's almost too late. I had a client recently who asked me if people her age (she is in her fifties) really needed wills or trusts. I can tell you that there are many who think like her – she's not the exception, but rather the rule. It's not easy to think or talk about death and dying but as we all know, it's something that we have to face sooner or later.

Some people think that if they have a will, they have an estate plan. While a will does provide instructions for distributing assets to your family and other beneficiaries, it does **not** avoid probate. This is an essential fact to consider and a strong reason to have a Living Trust as well as a will, no matter the size of your estate. Probate incurs costly legal fees and can take months or years to complete. In addition, probate documents are public so there is no privacy once your estate goes into probate. A will allows you to appoint someone to be an executor to pay final expenses, taxes, etc. and then distribute your remaining assets. If you have minor children, you can also designate a guardian for them. A will doesn't take effect until you die and it can't provide for management of your assets if you become incapacitated. That's why it's so necessary to have other estate planning documents like a living trust, health directive and power of attorney in place which become effective if you are unable to take care of your affairs.

Judy was a thirty-year old mother of two young children, ages 3 and 5. Her husband Paul, a prominent plastic surgeon, was about 20 years older than her. He was tragically killed in a plane crash flying home from a medical conference. Judy and Paul lived a very comfortable life and Judy naturally assumed that she and the children would be taken care of in the event of Paul's death. But in the midst of her grieving, she found out that Paul left only a will – no trust had been set up. In addition to having substantial personal assets, Paul was also a partner in a successful medical practice. There was no succession plan or buyout agreement in place. You can imagine the legal nightmare that Judy had to go through and the end of a very sad story is that it took eleven years and lots of legal costs to settle probate. Had Paul had a trust and business succession plan in place, all that could have been avoided.

As I mentioned earlier, putting an estate plan in place is something that we all naturally put off. When you consider all the important decisions that have to be made and all the documents you need to gather, you would probably rather just put the task aside and have a glass of wine instead. I've put together a list of what you'll need to have a good estate plan and I've also included all the decisions, answers and documents you'll need before you meet with an estate planning attorney. Yes, it's cheaper to download forms and take care of much of this online, but even if you choose this route, it would be worth the investment to have an attorney look over what you've put together.

A good estate plan should contain the following:

1. A will.

2. A revocable living trust to transfer and distribute your assets. While you are alive, you have full control of your assets and because the trust is revocable, you can make changes anytime you choose. By transferring assets into a revocable living trust, you can manage your financial affairs during your lifetime and provide management of those assets if you become incapacitated. A revocable living trust avoids probate, keeps personal information private, and can designate the disposition of trust assets to whomever you designate. There are many different kinds of trusts which are usually put in place to minimize estate taxes. Each trust has its own benefits and should be discussed with your attorney. There are marital trusts, charitable trusts, generation-skipping trusts, bypass trusts, testamentary trusts, qualified terminable interest property trusts, and so on.

3. A durable power of attorney is a document designating who will handle your business affairs and healthcare decisions if you are disabled or unable to act on your own. A power of attorney is a legal document in which you name another person to act on your behalf. You can give this person broad or limited powers depending on what is specified in the document. You should choose this person carefully because he or she will be able to sell, invest and spend or distribute your assets. A *traditional* power of attorney terminates upon your disability or

death. A *durable* power of attorney continues during incapacity and terminates upon your death.

4. A power of attorney for health care. A health-care power of attorney authorizes the person you designate to make medical decisions for you in the event you are unable to do so yourself. This document is necessary to avoid family conflicts and even court intervention should you become unable to make your own health care decisions. A "living will" details your wishes regarding the use of life-sustaining measures in the event of a terminal illness. It says what you want done and what you don't want done but doesn't give any individual the legal authority to speak for you. That is why it is usually coupled with a health-care power of attorney.

5. A form listing all your assets and where they are located.

6. A list of how you want your assets distributed. Have this discussion with your spouse and your attorney, or an appropriate family member, trustee, etc.

7. A "Do not Resuscitate", or DNR, medical order written by a doctor. It instructs health-care providers not to perform cardiopulmonary resuscitation (CPR) if a patient's breathing stops or if the patient's heart stops beating. Some feel this is an important document while others don't but it's always best to discuss this with the person you have chosen to be your health care advocate.

8. Naming a guardian for your minor children.

9. A discussion with your accountant/CPA and attorney as to the tax consequences of your estate plan.

10. Letters to your spouse and family. Consider writing a letter to your spouse or family regarding your wishes should you need to be removed from life support. Even if you have a living will, a personal letter from you will make it so much easier for them.

There are 5 essential documents you should have regardless of what your estate is worth or what phase of life you're in....

Will - A Will is the method most commonly used to transfer assets at your death. However, even with explicit instructions, this method has to go through the probate courts which can be costly and time-consuming. Plus, your will then becomes a public document. There are ways to avoid probate which we'll discuss in more detail further on.

Living Trust – One of the ways to avoid probate is by having a Living Trust and it would be the recommended way to transfer your assets at death. There is more confidentiality, it's less costly, you have more flexibility and your wishes are less likely to be contested than with a probated will. If you do set up a trust, remember to fund it by transferring all your assets to the trust. If the assets are not in the trust, they'll have to go through probate.

Advanced Health Care Directive - This is a specific form signed and dated by you and preferably witnessed by a trusted person, that lists your healthcare preferences to be used only if you're not able to communicate your wishes directly. It puts your family, doctor and the hospital on notice as to what treatment or care you would want or not want. It also gives authority to the person/s you select to make those decisions on your behalf.

Financial Power of Attorney - This form appoints one or more persons that you trust to handle your financial affairs should you be unable to do so yourself. An "immediate" or "durable" power of attorney allows your agent to immediately act on your behalf. A "springy" power of attorney goes into effect only when you are incapacitated.

HIPAA Release Form – Several years ago, the HIPAA regulation took effect which helped protect our healthcare information. By having this special form completed ahead of time, you allow those persons named in your advanced health care directive or power of attorney to have access to your healthcare information in order to deal with insurance matters on your behalf.

Avoiding probate

Other ways of avoiding probate include titling assets so that they are jointly owned by you and another person. Most common are:

1. **JTWROS** – Joint Tenancy with Right of Survivorship – this is the most common way a married couple titles their real-estate assets. Upon the first death, the property is transferred to the surviving spouse.

2. ***POD and TOD*** – Payable on Death and Transfer on Death, respectively. PODs are used for bank accounts and TODs are used for brokerage accounts. You add someone's name onto your account and upon your death, the cash or securities are transferred directly to that person without having to go through probate.

Estate planning documents are of no use until they are signed, dated and in some cases, witnessed. Most good planners will work with attorneys and have a process in place to help clients get their documents signed and make sure the trusts are funded. Regardless of where they are stored, it's best to have photocopies of the documents in a safe place or with a trusted relative or friend. The executor of your estate should have copies of your estate planning documents. I advise my clients to review their documents once a year and update or make changes as significant events like marriage, death or a new family member, occur in their lives.

Choosing an attorney

Estate planning is also like a team sport where attorneys, financial advisors, accountants, insurance brokers and other professionals work together to make sure your needs are met. It's important to build a cohesive team who can communicate with each other, work together and meet periodically to accomplish your objectives. Those of us with business entities or blended families need to make sure that our corporate or business attorneys and our family law attorneys communicate with our estate planning attorneys. Just as we'd like our internist to know what our cardiologist or other medical specialist is doing or has recommended for our physical well-being, it's important that all our various legal specialists are aware of our overall plan as well. When looking for an estate planning attorney, it's a good idea to ask them for two or three references of similarly situated clients with whom you can speak. Ask these references about the costs and timeline for completing a basic plan and estimated costs when extra work is necessary. And always ask if they received good service and good value for the money.

Having an estate plan prepared can be like a remodeling project in your house and hiring an attorney involves much the same process as hiring an interior designer or a contractor. If you pay too little, you may end up with shoddy work that will cause problems down the road. While remodeling, you might find that once a wall is opened, there may be lots of surprises that require additional work and costs. This can be the same when you start to put your estate plan in place. We'd all like to save money, but be realistic about your expectations in terms of service and quality. All estate plans are different and a well-prepared plan may cost a bit more upfront, but will save you and your heirs a great deal in the long-run.

Choosing an Executor

An executor is the person or persons named in your will to carry out your wishes after you die. This is a very important function that involves much responsibility so think carefully and choose the right person. I always advise my clients not only to ask the person for permission but also to describe in detail the responsibilities involved because an executor does have a right to refuse the position. Sometimes an executor can be a family member, but in many cases they can be a friend, an attorney or your financial advisor. It's a complicated job even if your estate is a simple one because the executor decides when to sell your property so that your heirs get as much money as possible. They also need to make sure that inheritance and estate taxes are paid in full, settle any outstanding debts, and use estate funds to pay for funeral and burial expenses. Estate planning attorneys work closely with executors to make sure the estate is settled properly and the assets are distributed to the beneficiaries.

Anyone over the age of eighteen can be an executor and there is no reason not to choose one of your beneficiaries as the executor – in fact, this is very commonly done. It's a good idea to choose two executors in case one of them dies before you. I also believe it's a good idea to have two executors, especially when one is a family member. The other can be your attorney, another professional or a friend who is familiar with your personal financial situation. Professional executors tend to charge for their services but even a family member is entitled to some compensation if they choose.

If you have minor children (under the age of eighteen), you'll also need to appoint a guardian to care for them in the event you and your spouse die at the same time. I don't need to go into detail to tell you how important this decision is, so think carefully and choose the right person. Again, always ask permission beforehand so that the person you choose is aware of the responsibility involved.

Chapter 8
Invest in Education

Maybe you have a college education and are thinking of continuing for a graduate degree in a specialized field. Or you have children and need to start planning and saving for their education. Or you're a stay-at-home Mom who would like to take courses to update your skills if or when you return to work. Whatever the reason, it's never too early to start thinking about funding your educational goals and it's wise to maintain your skills to stay current. Education is the great equalizer where employment is concerned today.

If you want to become financially independent and have control of your own money, you need to acquire and maintain the skills and experience to stay relevant in the work force. While you're actively working, this is not necessarily an issue. It becomes an issue when you take time off to raise children or become a caregiver. It also becomes an issue if you haven't worked for a long while and you suddenly find yourself widowed or divorced without enough money to maintain your lifestyle. During the time you're not working, try to take courses in a field that interests you. Or volunteer at an organization that can use the experience you acquired while you were working.

Even with ever increasing tuition costs and drop-outs who become multi-billionaires, a college education is still one of the best investments a person can make for themselves or a loved one. The Federal Reserve Bank of New York estimates that a bachelor's degree typically increases a person's earning capacity by about $300,000 (in today's dollars) over his or her working life.

Education planning is one of the key components of a good financial plan. It you want the best for yourself or your children, then a gift of education is priceless.

There are so many ways to take courses today – community colleges, university extension courses, life-long learning programs, online courses and so much more. Decide what type of work you'd enjoy or excel at... maybe you have a passion in a certain area. Sometimes your passion can become your profession too – and earn you a paycheck!

Funding Sources

Think about whether a private or a public college or university would be the best for you or your child. Once you've decided on where you'd like to go or what you'd like to study, start looking for the free money! Seriously, it's never too early to start looking at all the scholarships and grants that are available out there. These are gifts – they don't need to be repaid. There are thousands of grants and scholarships offered by schools, employers, individuals, private companies, non-profit organizations, religious groups and professional and social organizations. The best place to learn about these programs is to check with the financial aid office of the school you'd like to attend. You can also contact a high school college counselor, your local library, community groups or research Fortune 500 companies to find out if they offer education grants. The process may seem onerous at first, but the potential rewards make it all worthwhile.

Grants and scholarships come with no strings attached as long as you use the money for college-related expenses. Obviously, if you are very wealthy, you won't need help in financing an education. But you have nothing to lose by applying for financial help and you're not obligated to take the package offered if you don't want it.

Financial aid formulas are more concerned with your income than your assets; they don't expect you to sell your home to pay for an education. The formulas used for financial aid take into account your current life situation, so you can reapply every single year if necessary. The website FinAid.org will give you more details on how to apply.

Grants and scholarships are often used interchangeably but they are different in that grants are typically "need-based," which means they are awarded to students who really need the money to pay for their education. Scholarships, on the other hand, are often called "merit-based," because they are given out based on your academic achievement, athletic ability, career interest or ethnicity. Sometimes scholarships can be awarded based on financial need as well.

Grants are normally awarded by the federal government and by the individual states. The biggest grant program in the country is the Department of Education's Pell Grant but there are a number of others as well.

Businesses, non-profit organizations, religious groups and professional organizations are also big sources of educational grants. These grants are often awarded to students who intend to pursue careers associated with their mission or business. Colleges and universities also award grants, often

ELIZABETH SAGHI

through private endowments set up by wealthy individuals or businesses. So look around for the free money and financial aid before applying for student loans, which often carry a high interest rate.

529 Plans

As early as possible, start with a savings plan for your education, or especially if it's for your child. One of the most popular savings plan is the 529 plan which came into existence about 25 years ago and has grown tremendously in popularity. It is a tax-advantaged investment vehicle that helps you set aside money for future college costs. A 529 plan is operated by the state or a particular school and is similar to a retirement savings plan, like the 401(k). It can be used for yourself, your child or anyone you choose to help – you can name anyone as a beneficiary, including yourself, and you can change the beneficiary at any time. You make contributions that grow tax-deferred and the funds can be invested in mutual funds or individual stocks and bonds. The website SavingforCollege.com will give you details on 529 plans in all 50 states.

There are two types of 529 plans – savings plans and prepaid plans.

1. Savings plans allow you to choose from a variety of mutual funds and the amount saved is based upon the performance of those investments. The funds offered are age-based and become more conservative as the beneficiary gets closer to starting college. Contributions to 529 plans are considered gifts for tax purposes. In 2016, the annual gift exclusion is $14,000, so you can give that amount to anyone you choose without incurring a gift tax. You can actually give more in a 529 plan, but any amount over $14,000 in one year to an individual, even if it's a family member, will be considered a gift and therefore, subject to gift tax.

2. A prepaid plan can be administered by the state or by the specific college or university and allows you to purchase tuition credits at today's rates to be used in the future. Currently, only 10 states provide prepaid plans – Florida, Illinois, Maryland, Massachusetts, Michigan, Nevada, Pennsylvania, Texas, Virginia and Washington. Be aware that even though you can get your money back, there might be penalties if your child decides not to attend the school you've chosen and the money you invested may not have increased.

Your income potential is your greatest asset when you start out in your career. Investing in education and learning new skills on an ongoing basis makes you more valuable to an employer or if you are the employer, makes you a better role model for your employees. Focus on what you really want from your life – don't end up doing work that pays well but makes you miserable. Finding a balance between what you love and what will pay the bills can be challenging at times, but it's a great goal to pursue. Once you find your passion, try to determine what you need to do to earn more money from that passion. Ultimately, this will lead to a happy and productive life.

And finally, try not to use your retirement funds to pay for an education. You can get loans, grants and scholarships to put you or your children through college but unfortunately, no one wants to give you a loan to fund your retirement. There can also be tax consequences when you take money out of a qualified retirement plan to pay for college tuition. The message I'd like to leave you with here is that education is important, no matter what phase of life you're at – there's always something to learn.

Chapter 9
Thinking of Divorce or a Relationship Change?

When we fall in love and marry, the last thing we want to think about, much less talk about, is divorce. But sadly, it happens in about half of all marriages, so it's wise to prepare beforehand, just in case. If you're one of the lucky ones to have a long, happy marriage then nothing was lost. But money issues are the number one cause for divorce. We worry about infidelity from our partner, but financial infidelity can be as painful and so much more destructive. So plan for the worst but hope for the best.

The decision to divorce is one of the most crucial decisions a person can make because of the consequences that can last for years, or a lifetime. Many women stay in bad marriages because of money. I think one of the biggest fears women have is the "bag-lady syndrome." I've known many women with plenty of money to have this fear because there is always the possibility that they could "lose it all." I'm here to tell you that good planning will mitigate those fears.

Each state has different laws regarding community property process, spousal support and other issues surrounding divorce. Even if you're happily married, take the time to know what your legal spousal rights are in your state.

My clients, Terry and Jim, were married for 58 years before Jim died. For the most part, they had a good marriage but like many relationships, they went through a tough period right after their 40th anniversary. Toni was distraught and thought about leaving Jim, but she had always been a stay-at-home wife and mother and had no idea how she could support herself at age 67. She said that she had very little in her own name and though their bank and investment accounts were held jointly, she always felt it was Jim's money because he had earned it. I tried to explain to her that California laws entitled her to half of everything they owned jointly, but she was skeptical. So I suggested she consult an attorney to learn what her legal rights were in the event she chose to leave Jim. After several meetings, she felt much more comfortable knowing that even though Jim earned the money during their marriage, she was entitled to receive her share of their assets and spousal support as well. In the end, she stayed with Jim and they were able to resolve their issues. But I always believed that, from then on, she felt much stronger in their relationship knowing that she could leave if she chose and wouldn't be left destitute.

If you haven't done so already, make a list of your assets and how they are titled, i.e. whether you own them jointly or separately. This would include your home, other real-estate, life insurance policies, cars, artwork, furniture etc. It's a good idea to revisit this list periodically to update it with new acquisitions or those that have been sold or given as gifts. Think about dividing your marital estate at the same time as you are building one. Don't feel guilty or mercenary about this exercise – think of it as being prudent and prepared for any eventuality. This way, you'll have a good idea of how assets should or could be divided in case you separate or divorce.

Just as our spouses might hide some assets, they may not disclose their debt either. Know your partner's credit history – hopefully before marriage – but definitely after and during your relationship, as credit histories are always evolving. It's important to know that we marry our spouse's debt and we inherit that debt in death or divorce. Yes, even if you're divorced and your ex-spouse defaults on a loan, you are liable for the payments too. If you've been able to communicate openly about finances and you are both involved in the decision-making process throughout your marriage or relationship, then you probably have no need to be concerned. But if not, then now would be the time to begin.

Pre-nuptial and post-nuptial agreements

Of course, one of the best ways to plan for the possibility of a divorce is a pre-nuptial or post-nuptial agreement. A "pre-nup" basically establishes the property and financial rights for each spouse in the event of divorce. This is especially recommended if either of you has significant assets that you acquired through your own efforts before the marriage or through an inheritance. I see many of my clients wrinkle their noses when I mention 'pre-nups' because they feel it's like telling their fiancé or partner that they don't trust them or they don't feel one hundred percent committed to the relationship. But these agreements are especially important in financially unequal marriages or if one or both of you have children from a former marriage. They also preserve the expectations on both sides and avoid surprises if divorce should happen. In most cases, a court will uphold a pre-nuptial agreement. The only issues that shouldn't be included in a pre-nup are child custody and child visitation rights, for obvious reasons.

Community Property

Community property is the process by which most property acquired during the marriage is owned jointly by both spouses and divided only upon divorce, annulment or death. Gifts and inheritances are not considered community property unless they are commingled with other assets or funds that are jointly owned. If you are fortunate enough to receive an inheritance, think carefully before commingling that money with your partner or spouse. As long as you don't "mix" the money with jointly owned funds or buy a jointly owned asset, that money will always be your separate asset. If money is commingled, the person commingling must then prove and trace the source of money when assets have to be separated. If it can't be proven, then that asset is considered community property. All property acquired through work efforts during the marriage is considered community property. Check the laws of the state in which you reside to determine community property laws. There are nine community property states in the U.S. (Arizona, California, Idaho, Louisiana, Nevada, New Mexico, Texas, Washington and Wisconsin). Forty states are deemed "equitable distribution" and Alaska is considered an "opt-in" state, giving both spouses the option to make their assets community property.

There is a natural tendency for people who are in difficult marriages to want to get the divorce over with as quickly as possible in order to move on with their lives. I did that many years ago and I regret it to this day because I left a lot on the table, unnecessarily. Couples who make rushed decisions to leave the marriage have had no time to evaluate their feelings, thoughts or options. As a result, they are unprepared for the roller coaster of emotions, the complicated legal system and the many life-changing decisions that need to be made. Quite often, agreements are made that cannot be sustained and one set of problems has just been traded for another. If you can afford it, seek the counsel of a good divorce attorney and don't rush into anything.

Spousal Support

I live in California and I know that the main difference between this state and most others is that they are very generous with spousal support, especially for women. If you're in a situation where you think you'll need spousal support in your divorce settlement, the main issue to be concerned with is getting lifetime support orders. Many women don't realize that if their ex-spouse dies, retires or becomes disabled, the support may stop. I would also suggest that, if you're working, don't quit your job just because you're receiving spousal support, unless it's absolutely necessary. Spousal support orders can be challenged and changed and therefore, the initial order you received may not be the last one.

Nearing Retirement

For those of you who are divorcing at an age where you'll be retiring soon, time is of the essence to thoroughly analyze your financial situation so that you can be ready to retire and maintain your lifestyle as best you can. Remember that once you're divorced, you will be a one-income household and most likely that will mean making financial adjustments to your budget. Unwinding a marriage is a very stressful event but ensuring a comfortable retirement is one of our most pressing concerns.

Receiving part of an ex-spouse's pension or retirement plan is negotiated during the divorce settlement proceedings. However, you might also be entitled to Social Security benefits based on your ex-spouse's employment and he doesn't even have to know about it. If your ex-spouse is eligible for Social Security benefits and your marriage lasted ten years or longer, you can claim the higher of the benefits to which you're entitled or half of your ex-spouse's benefits, as long as you wait until your full retirement age to claim them. You must be unmarried at the time you claim your ex-spouse's benefit. I have come across a number of women who didn't know that they were entitled to what is referred to as the Divorced Spousal Benefit. Check with your advisor or the Social Security office to determine if you are entitled to this benefit and if it's advantageous for you.

Before making a commitment to marry or live with someone, you should discuss the following questions together:

- Who will handle the monthly bills?
- Will we combine our financial resources?
- Will we have separate bank and investment accounts?
- Am I a saver or a spender? Is my partner a saver or a spender?
- What is my credit score? What is my partner's credit score?
- Do either of us have outstanding debt we should discuss?

Talking about these issues honestly will save you much grief during your marriage because financial problems are one of the main reasons for divorce or separation.

Chapter 10
Working with an Advisor

From budgeting, planning for retirement, saving for an education, managing your taxes, investing your money, protecting your estate – it's all about having a good financial plan.

Nobody cares more about your money that you do but bringing all the pieces of your financial life together can be a challenging task. You may want to seek help from a professional when:

- You want to manage your finances better, but aren't sure where to start

- You don't have the time or inclination to do your own financial planning

- You want a professional opinion about the plan you've developed

- You need more expertise in certain areas, such as investments or estate planning

- You have an immediate need or an unexpected life event

A good financial advisor should help guide you throughout your financial life, keep you focused on your goals and help you implement changes when necessary. They can navigate you through the emotional highs and lows of various market dynamics so that you avoid the "Buy high, sell low," syndrome. Your advisor can facilitate the decisions you need to make as you move from one phase of your life to another, helping to determine your priorities and creating the roadmap to achieve your goals.

As a financial planner, money is my world. But in the broader culture and particularly with women, talking about money from a personal perspective can be difficult. The number one cause of stress in the lives of the majority of Americans today is money – it's a deeply emotionally charged subject. If someone doesn't have much, they're afraid they'll be judged a loser. If they have a lot, they fear others will try to take advantage of them. We all have different attitudes toward money. In Appendix II, you'll find a short quiz titled "What's Your Money Personality?" It was developed by the Alliance of Comprehensive Planners, of which I am a member, for use by financial planners with their clients. It might give you and your advisor more insight about your feelings towards money and help you develop a plan that mitigates your fears or enhances your positive attitudes.

The financial services industry deliberately makes their products sound more complex than they need to be. We all know how mutual fund prospectuses or insurance industry documents make our eyes glaze over when we have to read all their "fine print." And many of us are familiar with the foot-high pile of papers that need to be signed before our lender will approve a loan or mortgage. Just as we search for the right doctor or dentist, it's important to interview several financial advisors and find the one you feel understands your situation and needs best. Don't ever feel reluctant to ask, "I don't understand what you mean. Can you please explain it further?" Believe me, as an advisor, I would much rather have tons of questions thrown at me so that my clients understand fully what we're discussing. If you understand the pros and cons of every recommendation or option an advisor suggests, you're able to make much more informed decisions.

Industry Designations

Anyone can call themselves a financial advisor but there are industry designations and certifications that denote additional training, rigorous examinations and experience in the field. There are over 200 designations available for financial professionals today and you can find the complete list on the FINRA (Financial Industry Regulatory Authority) website at www.finra.org. All of the professionals holding these designations must meet annual continuing education credits as well. Here are a few of the more common designations that you'll come across:

CFP - Certified Financial Planner – Although many professionals call themselves "financial planners," CFP professionals have completed extensive training and experience requirements and are held to fiduciary standards.

CPA – Certified Public Accountant - Accounting professionals in the U.S. receive the CPA certification when they have passed the three-day Uniform Certified Public Accountant Examination and met additional state and experience requirements.

CFA – Chartered Financial Analyst – Investment and financial professionals receive this credential after a rigorous three-year study course with an exam given after each year. CFAs are usually investment analysts and/or money managers.

ChFC – Chartered Financial Consultant – Professionals who have completed an educational program and passed ten exams covering financial planning, investments and insurance and have also met experience and ethical standards.

EA – Enrolled Agent. A designation is awarded by the IRS to persons who wish to represent their clients before the IRS. They must pass a comprehensive, two-day exam on all aspects of tax law, including filing procedures.

Fee only vs. fee-based advisors

Many financial advisors in the U.S. today work for banks, brokerage firms or insurance companies and are compensated with commissions for selling a financial product or service or by managing your money. A lesser known, but growing alternative is the "fee-only" financial advisor who charges an hourly rate, a project fee or a retainer fee. These advisors are compensated solely for their time – not by commissions. Fee-only planners usually have a holistic business model in that they address every aspect of your financial situation, not just your investment accounts. They are a good fit for someone who wants an unbiased perspective on managing their assets, reviewing their retirement goals and estate plans, and generally providing ongoing advice to help you achieve your financial objectives. To find a fee-only planner in your area, go to the NAPFA (National Association of Personal Financial Advisors) website at www.napfa.org.

Commission based advisors are compensated when they sell investment or insurance products. Most of the time, the sales charges or fees are built right into the investment that is recommended so you may not even see them. Be aware of these fees, however, because they can reduce the overall return of your investment. For example, if you invest $25,000 into a mutual fund or an annuity with a sales charge of 5%, you are really only investing $23,750. If you hold that fund for ten years and the annual return is 5%, you'll have $38,686 versus $40,722 if you had invested in something that didn't cost you 5% upfront. That's a difference of $2,036. It's always advisable to know what the fees and expenses are before committing to any investment.

Wealth management firms usually charge a fee based on the percentage of assets that they are managing for you, typically one percent on an annual basis. Again, be aware of the fees charged because if the annual return the managers are generating on your investment portfolio is six percent your return is actually only five percent, after their fees are deducted. Generally, wealth management advisors have a "minimum" requirement of assets that are needed before they will take you on as a client, usually beginning at one million dollars.

A growing number of advisors are using the "hourly-only" fee model. They charge for their financial planning and advisory services, but receive no commissions or sales fees based on the amount you invest or the specific investments you choose. In actuality, you're paying for their services based on the amount of time they spend helping you. What matters most is the advisor you feel most comfortable with and not how much or how they are paid. You need to know the value of the professional advice you're receiving and decide what is best for you. But whatever the fee structure, you should always demand transparency, objectivity and honesty.

What is a Fiduciary?

The Department of Labor recently issued a new ruling that mandates all financial advisors be "fiduciaries" when advising clients on their retirement portfolios. I believe all financial advisors should act in a fiduciary capacity anytime they are advising clients in any aspect of their financial life, not just with their retirement accounts. Here's the difference:

- A fiduciary always acts in their client's best interest.
- Non-fiduciaries simply need to recommend a "suitable" investment for their clients.

The difference is that two investments that are essentially alike can carry different expenses and sales charges. A fiduciary would recommend the investment with the lower sales charge because that would be in their client's best interest. The other investment might be "suitable" but in the long run, would cost the client more because of the higher sales charges. This new ruling is the first step to providing better protection and transparency for clients and has raised pubic awareness about the standards of investment advisors. The financial industry is moving toward fee-based planning and selling on commission is becoming more difficult.

The most important qualities to look for in an advisor are loyalty, accuracy and efficiency. Advisors should be working for you to help you achieve your financial goals, not just get a better return on your portfolio. Every financial advisor should be motivated to provide the highest level of care to each and every client – it's simply the right thing to do.

Chapter 11
Planning for Your Peace of Mind

What does a financial plan look like?

I frequently get asked the question, "What does a financial plan actually look like? A comprehensive plan is customized to gather and analyze your personal data so that recommendations can be made to meet your specific financial goals. The following is what you should expect in a comprehensive financial plan:

- A summary of your personal data and financial goals
- A statement of your total net worth – what you own and what you owe
- A cash flow statement of all the income and expenses of your household
- A review of your insurance policies to make sure you and your assets are protected
- A review of your most recent tax returns to determine if taxes can be minimized now and in the future

- A review of your estate planning documents, if you have them, including your will, trust/s, health directives and any durable powers of attorney.
- A review of your retirement accounts, including any employer provided plan, IRAs etc.
- A review of your investment accounts with an asset allocation model

Your financial plan should include a summary and analysis of the above mentioned items. It should also include action recommendations with a timeline to implement any changes that are necessary. Sometimes the thoroughness of a comprehensive financial plan and the recommendations can seem overwhelming. But a good plan should be designed to put you at ease, not cause you to become anxious. So an option would be to build up your plan, one step at a time, based on the priorities of your goals and needs. For example, if estate planning is your immediate priority, then tackle that area first. Then go on to your next objective until you have put together a comprehensive plan that suits you perfectly. Financial planning is an ongoing process and you should take whatever time is necessary to understand the data and the recommendations being made. Most importantly and I know I'm repeating myself, review and monitor the plan on a regular basis.

Common life events that would necessitate changes in your financial plan:

- New job or promotion
- Receipt of an inheritance
- Change in marital status
- New child or grandchild
- Major investment gains or loss
- Health concerns

- Changes in beneficiary/s of retirement plans or insurance policies
- Sale or purchase of a home
- Sale or purchase of other major assets
- Death of a family member
- Retirement
- New business start-up or acquisition
- Gain/Loss of a business partner

Personal Records to keep

Keep a record of the following in a safe place, but make sure that someone you trust knows where to find this information.

1. Bank accounts – Name of institution, account number, type of account
2. Insurance Policies – car, house, life, health. Company name, policy numbers, date of policy, beneficiary/s
3. Investment accounts – Institution name, type of account, account number, location of any certificates held by you personally, advisors' name, address and phone number
4. Real-estate holdings – (documents for each property should be held separately)

   Deeds, mortgage records, receipts and records for any improvements
5. Safety deposit box – bank name, address, key number, location of key, box contents, those having access to the box
6. Retirement accounts – Type of account, name of custodial institution, beneficiary/s
7. Business holdings – Type of business, location, title in which business ownership is held. Any records such as

deeds, loans, mortgages, capital purchase receipts and improvements

8. Estate planning documents – Will, trust documents, health directive, financial power of attorney, records of gifts made during your lifetime

9. Personal loans outstanding – Person owed, amount owed, loan agreement or IOU, and date the loan is due

10. Tax returns for the last seven years

11. Names and phone numbers of your professional advisors, including your CPA, Attorney, CFP, Executor of your estate and the Trustee of your estate

Putting together a financial plan might sound daunting when you think of all the information that needs to be compiled and analyzed before the plan can be implemented. I will admit that the first plan you put together will take some time and effort. If you work with a planner, they will ask you for your most recent tax returns, insurance documents, banking and brokerage statements, any estate planning documents you may have, a list of your assets and a monthly cash flow statement. Depending on the complexity of your situation, other documents may be needed as well. But once the plan is developed and implemented, it's just a matter of fine tuning as events occur in your life that require changes. A plan can also be developed in stages, depending on what your immediate needs and priorities may be – it doesn't always have to be a comprehensive plan from the start. As you complete and add each section, it eventually becomes your comprehensive plan. And because change is a constant part of our daily lives, your plan should be monitored regularly and reviewed at least once a year.

So take it slowly, talk with your spouse or trusted family members before making important decisions. Think of a financial plan as your personalized financial GPS. It will help you know where you are, where you are headed and track your progress along the way. Remember that financial planning is an ongoing process and no decision is made that can't be changed or adjusted. It's your money and it's your life!

About the Author

Elizabeth Saghi is the Founder and President of InAlliance Financial Planning, a fee-only advisory firm based in Santa Barbara, California. She has over thirty years of experience in several different areas of the financial services industry. The first half of her career involved working with institutional clients for Merrill Lynch in New York and Bahrain, then with Credit Suisse and BNP-Paribas in London. She returned to the U.S. and joined a team at Morgan Stanley in San Francisco that provided retirement planning and financial literacy seminars to employees of some of the largest firms in the Bay Area, including Apple, Intel and McKesson.

Elizabeth also served as the Investor Relations consultant for small, public companies in the San Francisco Bay Area with the Financial Relations Board, now part of the Interpublic Group. After moving to Santa Barbara in 2004, she joined Santa Barbara Bank & Trust as Marketing Manager for their Commercial & Wealth Management Group. In 2013 she acquired her CFP (Certified Financial Planning) certification and founded InAlliance Financial Planning so that she could fulfill her dream of offering objective, fee-only financial advice to clients from all backgrounds, with a particular emphasis on helping women.

Elizabeth received her Bachelor's degree from Boston University and her Certificate of Financial Planning from the College of Financial Planning in Denver. She is a member of NAPFA (National Association of Personal Financial Planners), ACP (Alliance of Comprehensive Planners), and FPA (Financial Planning Association). She lives in Santa Barbara with her family and is very involved with several local non-profit groups, including the Breast Cancer Resource Center and the Pierre Claeyssens Veterans Foundation.

Connect with the Author

Email: esaghi@inalliancefinancial.com

Website: http://www.inalliancefinancial.com

LinkedIn: https://www.linkedin.com/in/elizabeth-saghi-cfp-3bb6359

Facebook: https://www.facebook.com/InAlliance-Financial-Planning-938216452934262/

In Appreciation...

Thank you for buying my book. I hope you have found it to be helpful and will use it as a reference guide while you prepare or revise your financial plan. I would welcome questions, comments or any feedback, which you can provide through a review on Amazon or email me directly at esaghi@inalliancefinancial.com

Appendix 1
Personal Cash Flow Statement and Net Worth Statement Forms

PERSONAL CASH FLOW STATEMENT

			MONTHLY	ANNUALLY
INCOME		Salary (1)		
		Salary (2)		
		Other (please specify)		
	INVESTMENT INCOME	Interest Income		
		Dividend Income		
		Rental Income		
		Other (please specify)		
		Total Inflow		
	SAVINGS	Reinvestment (interest/dividends)		
		401(k) plan deferrals		
		Educational funding		
		IRA funding		
		Other (please specify)		
		Total Savings		

1

PERSONAL CASH FLOW STATEMENT

EXPENSES	ORDINARY LIVING EXPENSES		MONTHLY	ANNUALLY
		Food	MONTHLY	ANNUALLY
		Clothing	MONTHLY	ANNUALLY
		Rent	MONTHLY	ANNUALLY
		Utilities	MONTHLY	ANNUALLY
		Child care/school fees	MONTHLY	ANNUALLY
		Home Maintenance	MONTHLY	ANNUALLY
		Auto Maintenance	MONTHLY	ANNUALLY
		Other (please specify)	MONTHLY	ANNUALLY
		Total living expenses	MONTHLY	ANNUALLY

2

115

PERSONAL CASH FLOW STATEMENT

			MONTHLY	ANNUALLY
EXPENSES	**DEBT PAYMENTS**	Credit Card Payments Principal		
		Credit Card Payments Interest		
		Mortgage Payment Principal		
		Mortgage Payment Interest		
		Other (please specify)		
		Total Debt Payments		
	INSURANCE PREMIUMS	Automobile Insurance		
		Homeowners/Renters Insurance		
		Life/Disability Insurance		
		Other (please specify)		
		Total Insurance Premiums		

3

PERSONAL CASH FLOW STATEMENT

EXPENSES

TAXES

	MONTHLY	ANNUALLY
FICA and federal income tax (W/H)		
State (and city) income tax		
Property Tax		
Total Taxes		
Total Expenses		
Discretionary Cash Flow (Negative)		

4

STATEMENT OF NET WORTH

ASSETS		LIABILITIES	
CASH	Checking Account	**CURRENT LIABILITIES**	Credit Card Balances Due
	Savings Accounts		Monthly Mortgage Payments
	Money Market Funds		Utility Bills Due
	Short-term CDs		Insurance Premiums Due
	Other (please specify)		Taxes Due
	Total Cash/Cash Equivalents		Medical Bills Due
			Repair Bills Due
			Total Current Liabilities
INVESTMENTS	Stocks		
	Bonds		
	Treasury Securities	**LONG-TERM LIABILITIES**	Principal Residence Mortgage
	Educational Fund		Vacation Home Mortgage
	401(k) Plans		Other Mortgages
	IRA/s (including ROTH IRAs)		Automobile Loans
	Other (please specify)		Home Improvement Loans
	Total Invested Assets		Student Loans
			Other Loans
PERSONAL USE	Principal Residence		**Total Long-Term Liabilities**
	Vacation Home		
	Automobile(s)		**TOTAL LIABILITIES**
	Jewelry/Furs		
	Art & Antiques		
	Furniture		
	Other (please specify)		
	Total Personal Use Assets		
	TOTAL ASSETS		**NET WORTH** (ASSETS - LIABILITIES)

Appendix 2
What's Your Money Personality* Quiz

* *Courtesy of The Alliance of Comprehensive Planners, a community of fee-only financial planners passionately dedicated to serving clients first.*

What's Your Money Personality?

Understanding our beliefs about money is important because these in turn direct our behavior with money, which is perhaps the most significant factor in determining whether or not we become financially successful.

Select the number that best matches your Risk Acceptance
1. The most important thing to do with my money is to keep it safe.
2. I believe a bird in the hand is worth two in the bush.
3. Risk-taking often makes me worry.
4. I am generally conservative when dealing with risk.
5. Sometimes I take risks and sometimes I play it safe.
6. I am generally aggressive when dealing with risk.
7. Sometimes I take risks on impulse.
8. I take big risks but choose them carefully.
9. I'm willing to take a lot of risk for the chance of a big financial reward.

Select the number that best matches your Saving/Spending Tendencies
1. I squeeze every penny I can out of my budget.
2. Use it up, wear it out, make do, or do without.
3. I am a very careful shopper and use coupons.
4. I buy quality and rely on brand names.
5. I save 10% of my income.
6. I like to pamper myself with little things.
7. I love to really splurge once in a while.
8. Life is short. Eat dessert first.
9. I spend every penny I get.

Plot your two numbers on the grid below:

MONEY PERSONALITY MATRIX

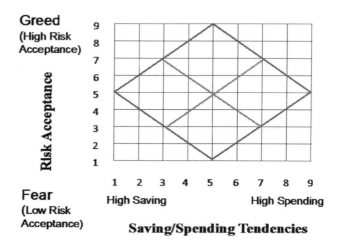

Find your money personality on the Money Personality Matrix below:

MONEY PERSONALITY MATRIX:
MORE COMMON FINANCIAL PERSONALITY TYPES

The Scrooge

Characteristics

- Strongly motivated to accumulate great wealth
- Strong propensity to save
- Often success business people
- Distrustful of others
- Very concerned with confidentiality
- Suspicious of all kinds of financial schemes
- Repeated the same money making technique over and over
- Controlling personality type

Issues

- Hate to pay taxes
- Surround themselves with "yes men"

The Gambler

Characteristics

- Strong desire to be associated with wealth
- Strong propensity to spend
- Heavy debt, IRS trouble
- Addictions
- Incorrigible optimistic
- Remorseful and depressed about choices/mistakes
- Crime activity to pay back debts
- Secretive about how they handle money

Issues

- Lie to themselves and others
- Brag about wins and deny losses
- Vulnerable to get rich quick schemes
- Warped logic that casino or horses races are investments
- Life insurance to counter mistakes

The Shopaholic

Characteristics
- Friendly, outgoing
- Give gifts, pick-up the tab (Compulsively)
- Shopping experience rituals
- Hate to keep records (evidence)
- Denial
- Don't know debt level
- Have enablers in their lives. Codependents funding the spending.
- Poor background, not deny kids what they did not have

Issues
- Jewelry as investment
- Purchase to get even with spouse/partner
- Credit card debt
- Addictive rituals in spending with triggers for shopping
- Experience shopping high, post purchase remorse
- Hide purchases
- Hoarding
- Least happy of personality types

The Miser

Characteristics
- Fear motivation
- Champion savers
- Put money in the "mattress"
- Avoid long term investments
- Childhood with high money consciousness
- Use insurance as an investment
- Not financially astute, inappropriate decisions

Issues
- Distrustful, tight with precious things
- Deny themselves pleasures

- Under spender
- Pay the IRS too much to avoid problems

The Nester

Characteristics
- Great savers
- Favorite investment is home
- Over improve their homes
- Family oriented often with strong religious ties
- Practical
- Proud of how they handle money

Issues
- Purchases for the home are "investments"
- Impulse to pay off mortgage as soon as possible
- Time share owner

The Entrepreneur

Characteristics
- Risk takers (may thrive on it)
- Workaholics engrossed in their business
- Child of business owners or had a business as a child
- Business is life purpose
- Use money to keep score

Issues
- Put all their money in their business
- If "diversified", likely to trade risky investments.

The Traveler

Characteristics
- Money an experience rather than things
- Anti-materialistic or proudly "downwardly mobile"
- Thrive on personal growth programs

- Professional students
- Professions that involve travel
- Like simple life and avoid stress and worry
- Photo album is a prized possession

Issues
- Perpetual self-growth journey
- Doesn't settle down

The Bon Vivant

(A person who enjoys a sociable and luxurious lifestyle)

Characteristics
- Workaholics-long hours, lots of money
- Dual income no kids
- Spend money on anything that saves them time (gadgets)
- Shop in catalogs or online
- Concerned with status and prestige

Issues
- Ad hoc investments
- Panic with market ups ands and downs
- Cocktail party investments
- Confuse hobbies with investments

Made in the USA
San Bernardino, CA
29 November 2016